# Mornings with Ron

*Messages to provoke thoughts,*
*inspire the heart,*
*and feed the soul*

ISBN: 978-0-578-66048-6
Library of Congress Control Number: 2020904626

Proofing by Proof Positive Papers
Book cover design by Michael Picco
Editing by Donna Hartman, Joe Maloney, and L. A. Wagner

First printing edition 2020.

Ron Tyson
P.O. Box 226
Odessa, FL 33556
www.morningswithron.com

# Mornings with Ron

*Messages to provoke thoughts,*
*inspire the heart,*
*and feed the soul*

## BY RON TYSON

# Contents

# Foreword

WHILE THE NEXT MINUTE that appears on your watch can be anything you want it to be, it is the past that often gives us the guidance we need to navigate our life path. Our life experiences and what we learn from those around us are often used as a compass for where we want our lives to go. No one person has all the answers, and the journey is different for each of us. However, there are things that we experience in our lives that can help others with their life path if we only take the time to share. That is the purpose of this book.

From an early age I loved to write. It was a passion that I never pursued as a career, but one that I hoped would one day lead me to this very moment. The messages in this book are meant to provoke thoughts, inspire the heart, and feed the soul. They are neither right nor wrong. They are simply my life experiences that I share with you in hopes that within these paragraphs you will find something that helps you make your life all it was meant to be.

One does not write a book without a multitude of people who support you in your journey to publishing. While my supporters are too numerous to mention, I do want to thank my mother and father, my family, and my friends for being my biggest cheerleaders. I would also like to thank my editors Joe Maloney, Donna Hartman, and Lori Wagner, my graphic designer, Michael Picco, and my proofer, Cindy at Proof Positive Papers. My heartfelt thanks also goes out to my Mah Jongg family, my Bring Smiles to Seniors family, and all those who believed in me and lifted me up through this process.

I hope as you read the words in this book that you will find something that resonates in your own life. If some message within these pages helps you make your life the best that it can be, then my work is done. Happy reading!

# Why I Write

ONE OF THE QUESTIONS I am asked most often is why I write. I am a firm believer that writing—like any other talent—is a gift, and gifts that aren't used and shared are often lost. People have so many talents they are often unaware of. Others recognize and develop their talents and make the decision to share them with the world. That is exactly what I choose to do.

At an early age, I had a passion for writing. When I was 10, I went to the five-and-dime store and bought myself a hardback ledger—the kind people used to keep track of accounts. I cut pictures out of magazines and pasted them on each page of the ledger. I wrote a poem about each one of the pictures and wrote about anything that I found stimulating and fun. I would spend hours at a time in my room writing poetry and stories.

The main reason I continued to write was because I was encouraged to do so. The importance of letting children be creative and express who they are through their abilities cannot be underestimated. I was very fortunate to have a family that let me do just that. They celebrated my talent, rather than discourage it, and were always there to read my latest work and provide feedback and encouragement. Never once did they stifle my creativity, and that gave me the passion to continue to write over the years.

There were several times when I attempted to write a book and I always got just so far and would either lose interest or reach a mental roadblock that prevented me from continuing. However, I always knew that I would find an outlet for my writing, where I could share it with others and, through this book, that has finally happened.

My first step toward achieving my goal was writing a blog. The problem was that no one read it, and I felt like I was writing to a ghost audience. Then I discovered that people could actually sign up to receive the posts regularly, and the magical match was made. I had an outlet to share my writing and stories, and that put me on the path to my ultimate desire.

My writings are never meant to convey that I know everything. That's certainly far from the truth. I write to share my experiences and feelings from my point of view. I write to provoke thoughts in the hope that my words may give someone a reason to think about something that may be going on in their life.

Do you have a gift or talent that needs exploring and sharing? If so, uncover it and ignite the passion for the talent inside you. When you find that passion, share it with others so they, too, can be encouraged to do the same. The ultimate answer to the question of why I write is simply this: I write because it is my way of sharing my gift with you.

# Getting Started

D<small>O YOU EVER HAVE THOSE</small> mornings when you wake up in bed and you just do not want to move from under the covers and plant two feet on the floor to get started? You had a good night's sleep, but for some reason the motivation just isn't there to take that first step and so you lie there just a little longer.

When that happens to me, and it often does, I try and focus on all the possibilities that lie in front of me. I tell myself that I have the gift of another day. I visualize what the day is going to bring, and often the excitement that begins to build is just what I need to motivate me to move.

When we wake up, we have many choices. Life is going to present us with many possible variations on how our day could go. The decisions we make regarding those variations determine what state we are in when we finally fall back into bed in the evening.

I always question why work weeks seem to drag and weekends and vacations fly by. In reality, every day has 24 hours or 1,440 minutes or 86,400 seconds. What we do with that gift of time ultimately leaves us feeling either satisfied or dejected once those minutes have passed. Often a slow start can wind up in a fast finish.

Everyone has a "down day" once in a while. It is the nature of being human in the crazy world we live in. But if we choose wisely throughout the day, we can avoid those down days and live a full, rich life. We won't waste the precious moments that we are given.

So, if you are feeling a little lethargic this morning, focus on the possibilities that the gift of this day may offer. Find one thing you can do, either big or small, that will make you feel good. Buy a coffee for the person in the car behind you. Write just one card to a friend or a senior. Take out the trash without having been asked. Or, simply phone a friend, remind them how much they are loved, and tell them what they mean to you. When you go to bed tonight, focus on the day and all the opportunities you were presented and evaluate the choices you made. Pat yourself on the back for making the most of the day and remind yourself that every day is truly a gift.

# Beauty Within

"Beauty is in the eye of the beholder" is an often-used phrase to say that beauty is subjective, meaning that beauty is defined depending on the circumstance and situation. Sometimes we don't think about what "real beauty" is.

Years ago, when I was in the Air Force, the Ms. Florida Association asked for a group of airmen to escort contestants at a beauty pageant in Tampa. It didn't take long for airmen to volunteer, and we arrived at the event. When we were ushered into the room where we would meet the ladies, we got quite excited. The doors opened, and there they were.

Who we met was not who you would have expected at a traditional beauty pageant. Yes, there were women of all ages in exquisite gowns, with beautiful hair and make-up. However, there was one difference: These women were in wheelchairs. We had been invited to be escorts in the Ms. Florida Wheelchair Pageant.

Immediately, we had to throw out societal norms and focus on the job at hand and were introduced to each woman we would be escorting for the night. Any thought that this night would be different than any other pageant quickly melted away as we each spoke and bonded with our assigned contestant. The beauty of their passion, their drive, and their acceptance that they were no different than anyone else resonated with all of us. The airmen were determined to do everything possible to help our contestants win.

As the pageant unfolded, I was impressed with the stories each contestant told in their prepared remarks. I was enthralled with their answers to questions they were asked. I was amazed by their poise, talent, and bravery as they embraced their situation and made their lives better for it. That was beauty personified.

Many people equate beauty with women they see on the covers of glamour magazines, models walking down a runway, or movie stars on the red carpet. They may all have features considered traditionally beautiful, but their external beauty doesn't encompass everything that beauty is.

Beauty comes from the heart. You realize this when you walk away from a person and you feel better for having been in their presence. You recognize genuine beauty when you interact with people who radiate goodness, caring, and compassion. True beauty emanates from inside you when you embrace who you are, love yourself, and strive to make the world a better place.

That pageant was a defining moment for me. I stayed in contact with my contestant for many years. She didn't win, but in my heart, she was a winner as was every woman who wheeled across that stage. Take a few moments today and remind yourself of your beauty. It's there… just embrace it and let it shine.

# A New Day

HAVE YOU EVER BEEN up at the time of morning when the dark blue of the night sky is starting to change to beautiful orange and purple as the sun starts to come up over the horizon? All that was still during the night starts to come alive. The horizon takes on a magical air with the excitement of a new day. If you are out and about, more and more cars travel the streets, the houses start to light up when people begin their morning routines, the streetlights start to go off, and suddenly a new world of opportunity emerges.

The beginning of a day is always exciting. We wake up with a clean slate and a chance to make the day anything we want it to be. Whether we have plans or we decide to be spontaneous, every minute of those hours we will be awake is full of potential to be something great.

Recently, I was sitting on the train, staring at my watch. As the second hand continued to tick, the obvious suddenly dawned on me: Every minute that passed was a minute I was never going to get back. I realized how incredibly important it was to make every minute matter. That's not saying that we don't need our downtime and rest. We could all surely use more of that. But I think I was recognizing the importance of making the most of the minutes where I am active and being aware of and honoring them in a way that makes life more meaningful.

A new day is a gift. Although it sometimes starts to go astray the minute we get up, we have the power within us to alter that course and make it our own. No one else can affect our day unless we give them that power. I am sure you have experienced the beauty of the morning at sunrise. If you haven't, you're missing something amazing. So set your alarm, take a step outside, and see the magic of a new day. Grab it by the reins and make it your own. Use the new day to make a promise to be good to yourself and make every minute count.

# Just Do It

COMMITMENT IS COMPLICATED. It is a mental agreement with yourself to do something and see it through. No one in the world has the power to make us commit to something except us, and if we spent as much time actually doing as we do talking, we would achieve success more often. Many of our commitments start with the best intentions, but often end with an unsatisfied goal and potentially a feeling of guilt. Imagine for a moment what might happen when we make a commitment and follow through.

Several years ago, I started walking in the mornings with my neighborhood friend, Linda. The reasons to be committed to my task were clear: I needed to lose some weight and find a way to prepare for a stressful day at work. I also had a desire to learn to run. At the age of 54, I knew I needed to work my way up to running, so I made the commitment to follow a process. Walking led to intermittent jogging and eventually I was able to run. Throughout the process, I was guided by a 5k training app that served as my support. The whole process started in the month of August, and by the following February I ran my first 5k race. You see, I'd had enough of saying "I'm going to" and found my way to "I will." The feeling of running by my family and friends during that race left me with a sense of satisfaction as I saw my commitment through.

Is there something you have been wanting to do for a long time? There is no better time to do it. To be successful, we must believe in ourselves, believe in what we want to accomplish, remove excuses from our thoughts, and never give self-doubt a chance to change our course. Make a true commitment, and when you least expect it, you too will be crossing the finish line.

# What Does Your Palette Look Like?

ONE OF MY FAVORITE THINGS about getting out of bed in the morning is that I get the chance to be a master artist. With my first foot on the floor, I am starting with a blank canvas that can be anything I want it to be. The choices of the past may have influenced how I got to this moment, but the choices I make from this minute forward will shape what my day, week, and eventually my life will become.

One of the things I focus on lately in my meditation is the importance of not letting the mistakes and bad choices that I have made affect the choices that I will make going forward. Growing is learning, and mistakes are a part of that process as we try our best to figure out this thing called life. Bad choices do not mean that we have a license to punish ourselves for the rest of our life. Good choices provide validation that we are on the right path and doing what is necessary to make our lives whole and fulfilled.

Equally important is not letting others step on the painting that we are trying to create. It is not theirs; it is ours. Their negativity and lack of support should not be used as an excuse for not making it the most beautiful picture it can be. While we can learn from our mistakes, dwelling on them and allowing them to be a primary color in our palette does us no justice.

As you work on your canvas today, take a good long look at your colors and decide what the painting is going to look like. Will your primary colors be blacks, grays, and other dark colors? Or, will you choose the vibrant colors that will shape the life you truly want and deserve?

# Do What You Love

ON A TRIP TO BRYANT PARK in New York City, I happened to glance across the street at a building where a flag was flying that said, "Do What You Love." Something so simple, yet so powerful just flying there in the breeze. It got me thinking.

As we go through life, we are presented with all kinds of choices: careers, relationships, hobbies, and a multitude of other things. How often are we making choices to do what we truly love? Doing what is comfortable is easy, whether it makes us happy or not. We expand on the quality of life when we stretch ourselves to get out of the mundane and focus on doing that which bring us joy.

Picture a life where we get up in the morning and we look forward to going to work. We turn over and adore the person lying next to us. We spend our free time doing things that thrill us while nurturing and enriching our lives. When we lay our head down on the pillow at night, we are content with what we have accomplished throughout the day and look forward to getting up the next morning and doing it all over again.

We always want the best for our family and friends. Why wouldn't we want the same for ourselves? Sometimes we may think that we don't deserve it. But we do. No one has an obligation to us more than the obligation we have to ourselves. Happiness and contentment are always in our hands, and we should make life the best that it can be.

We must live life, enjoy life, and love life. We only do that by making choices that make our lives better. No matter how old you are, it is never too late to make that one change that is going to make your life magical. We only get one life to make it all that it can possibly be, and tomorrow is never guaranteed. That is why it is so incredibly important to make life your own and do what you love.

# Do You Need a Vacation from Life?

WE ALL MAKE CHOICES ABOUT the different things that make up our life—our work, our friends, the activities we choose, and the people we select to go on life's journey with us. When you sit down and take a good look at those components, are the choices you are making filling your life with things that enrich it and make it enjoyable? Or, are you filling it with mundane tasks and people who in the end just make you want to take a vacation from it all because you really want something different?

We have absolute choice over the life we live. The problem is that sometimes even though we are in life situations that we don't like, we are so comfortable in the mire of it all that we either don't know how or just choose not to change it. We stay in bad jobs because we need the paycheck. We choose unhealthy relationships because we are afraid of being alone. Having someone, anyone is good enough. We involve ourselves in activities because it is what we are supposed to do, not because it is something we enjoy. We even get ourselves into situations because we don't know how to say no, even though it is something that has no positive impact on our life.

People who truly love their lives and live a life full of meaning and purpose on their terms are wonderful to be around. They have found the art of making choices in their life that fulfill and enrich it, while living a life for themselves rather than a life that someone else wants for them. It is not easy to live your own life, and there is an art to it. However, once you master it, the benefits are amazing. It doesn't happen overnight, and it is always a work in progress.

So, self-reflect and take an inventory of your life and evaluate what kind of life you have chosen for yourself. Will the things you do today be things that enrich your life and make it better? Or, will the activities and events you have chosen keep you living a life that causes a constant need for a vacation? The choice is ours. Will we make the right one?

# Yes, It Is Okay
# to Be Sad

D O YOU EVER HAVE DAYS when no matter how hard you try, you are just sad and somber? You can't seem to break out of it and then—in a flash—your dreary mood passes. Sometimes you can't really pinpoint a reason for gloominess, and there are times when the reason is obvious, but it seems to come and go unexpectedly.

For me that seems to happen about once every four to six weeks. For about a two-day period, I wake up feeling down and there seems to be no obvious cause. I try to shake myself out of it, but it continues for about 24 to 36 hours and then as quickly as it started, it ends.

This has been happening to me for some time, and when it first started happening, it startled me. I couldn't understand why it was happening regularly and why it always seemed to come within a certain time interval. However, as time went on, I learned to embrace that period for what it was and put it to good use.

Most of the time, I am positive about life and do what I can to make it the best it can be. Week after week, I keep going until I get to the point where I feel like my body and soul just need a rest. I have come to learn that these periods of somberness are my body and mind's way of telling me to stop and slow down. By enduring those sluggish times when I don't want to seem to do anything, my body and mind are telling me to just chill and recharge without having to worry about anything else. When I feel sufficiently rested, the mood lifts, and life moves on.

My point is that it's okay to be somber and sad for short periods of time. Those moments are healthy respites so we can deal with the things that adversely affect our lives. But when sadness continues for weeks, months, and even years, it starts to become an issue and a person may ultimately need help to address it.

So, the next time that you feel sad and down, put that emotion to good use. Use it as a time to deal with the things in your life that are contributing to making you feel that way. Take a good long look at them, work through them, and let them go. It will make all the other days of life that much brighter. Sadness is a normal human emotion, and yes, it is normal to occasionally be sad.

# Just a Little
# Too Late

HAVE YOU EVER HAD a moment in your life when you felt the need to do something and just never got around to it? Have there been times when you had the opportunity to do something and failed to make the effort because you were distracted from the task at hand? Then—suddenly—the opportunity was no longer there, and you were left regretting the fact that you never did what you knew you needed to do. One such case for me involved an aunt in my family.

One of my favorite people growing up was my Aunt Gail. I cannot even begin to count the hours we spent together talking, laughing, and just enjoying each other's company. She was much younger than my uncle, so that made her much closer to my age. She would come over and visit me for the weekend, and we would play cards and laugh and do all the things that made our relationship fun. We had been hanging out since I was in school, and we were as close as a brother and sister.

When I moved away from Florida, some unfortunate family drama occurred that resulted in Aunt Gail and I losing touch and going our separate ways. The letters and the calls stopped, and for a while we had no contact at all. She was always in the back of my mind, and I missed her, but given the circumstances, a continued relationship was not meant to be.

Through another aunt, I found out that Aunt Gail was living away from our hometown without my uncle. The other aunt let me know that Aunt Gail had been asking about me and wanted to see me. This seemed like the perfect opportunity to mend fences. Aunt Gail just had surgery and was recuperating at home, so when I got around to it, I knew I would be able to catch her. Unfortunately, several weeks went by without my making the call. Something always came up to prevent me from doing so, or in my mind I just wasn't ready. I am not sure which.

One afternoon, my other aunt called and asked me if I had connected with Aunt Gail. I told her that I had not contacted her yet, but that I would. She then informed me that it was too late as Aunt Gail had passed away the day before from complications from her surgery. My window of opportunity was gone, and I never got to make amends. I was utterly devastated that I had not taken the opportunity to do what I knew I needed to do when I could have.

It's understandable that things are going to happen in life that create conflict between individuals, even those you love. So why is it that we allow so much time to go by before we try to rectify the issue? Is it because we just aren't ready? Maybe it's because we simply can't swallow our pride and be the one who makes the first move. No matter what the reason, keeping the door closed until it is too late doesn't benefit us or the other person.

If there is someone in your life from whom you are estranged and you have a desire in your heart to make it right, today is the day to make that happen. Don't wait, as it is okay to be first. The last thing that you want is for it to be just a little too late.

# Learning to Appreciate What You Have

I T's EASY TO GO THROUGH LIFE and take what we have for granted. But the things we need for survival always seem to be there if we work to get them. Because of that, we assume that our needs will always be met. Mom and Dad always made sure we had food on the table. As an adult, I've had a job to provide for myself. But we find ourselves lulled into what can sometimes be a false sense of security when all it takes is one adverse event that can change everything.

When I left the Air Force in 1985, I left the security of the military. I was given housing, food, and medical care, and I never had to worry where my next meal was coming from. My paycheck arrived every month, and even if I spent it all, I still had a roof over my head and food in my stomach. When I left the military, I was suddenly faced with the reality that I had to pay rent, buy food, and take care of bills and all the things that come with living on your own. Trying to do that with a part-time job and realizing the sudden reality of having to take care of myself was unnerving.

There was a time when, after paying the bills, I did not have enough left for food. I would get up and go in my kitchen, and it would be completely bare. There were times I would go days without eating, which was not good for a 5'11" man with a 27" waist. Fortunately, my parents lived a few hours away. Although I hid the fact that I was going through this from them, I eventually told them, and I got a well-deserved tongue-lashing. When I visited them, they would make me go in their pantry and "go shopping" for food, and I would take bags of food with me when I went home.

Eventually, I got a full-time job and things turned around. This trying time was painful, but it was a lesson I do not regret. I learned the importance of appreciating what I had after experiencing what it was like to not have. I became more compassionate for people who struggle and find themselves without. My good friend Linda tells me all the time that she constantly gives thanks for the things she has. She gives thanks for her food, her health, her housing, her family, and all the blessings that have been bestowed on her. It's an important reminder to regularly take stock and do the same.

My hope is that no one ever experiences what I did to learn to appreciate life's blessings. Look at your life, and if you haven't shown appreciation recently for all that you have, make a point to do so. When we are thankful for what we have, we can sustain what we have and create room for more empathy for those who don't.

# Living in
# the Moment

WHY DO WE SPEND SO MUCH time focusing on what is coming next that we miss what is happening in the moment? We miss it because we are so busy thinking about tomorrow, next week, next month, or even next year. We are so worried about what is to come that we fail to enjoy what is right in front of us.

On a recent weekend with friends, I really made a conscious effort to be in and enjoy the moment—the conversation, laughter, sharing, and excitement of being with them. I did not write. I did not think about work. I did not even think about what was coming up for the next week. For that weekend, I just lived in the moment, and it was magical.

Life is often arduous given all the responsibilities we have. The things we can control often make it hard, while the things we have absolutely no control over make it even more difficult. We spend so much time planning and executing that spontaneous, enjoyable moments slip by, and we lose the opportunity to experience them. If we take the time to enjoy them, those unexpected moments can become experiences that have the possibility to create memories that last a lifetime.

I often hear others (and myself) say that they cannot believe how fast time is going by. If I look back over the recent past, I can point to events that happened that I sailed through without taking the time to just stop and be in the moment—events where I was so focused on what was going to happen that I failed to enjoy what was happening. It was for that reason that I began to make a conscious effort to be more present in every moment.

When we take the time to live in the moment, we learn new things about ourselves and others that may have been previously unknown. We see things we have never seen before. We gain new understandings about people and situations by taking the time to stop and think. We even create better friendships and relationships with new, more solid foundations.

If I think back to that weekend with my friends, I can remember every conversation and activity in detail. Two days seemed like a week vacation because I took the time to be present and enjoy. As you go through your day today, look for those same opportunities. Be present in the moment. Live life one minute at a time, as it was meant to be. That doesn't mean we can't plan. What it means is that we will not miss opportunities that arise that can make our lives even more special, all because we chose to live in the moment.

# Celebrate, Celebrate, Celebrate

ONE FRIDAY, I HAD THE OPPORTUNITY to celebrate a friend's 75th birthday in one of my favorite cities, New Orleans. Each year, I was invited to his birthday celebration on a Friday at Galatoire's Restaurant. It was always a wonderful event. To see the magic of being surrounded by family and friends as you celebrate another year of life is truly something special. This experience reminded me how important it is to enjoy those special moments.

As we go through life, we get many opportunities to celebrate special events. Holidays, birthdays, anniversaries, births, and more. Every one of these celebrations is a chance to be with family and friends and make memories that will last a lifetime. They provide us the opportunity to look back on these special occasions when our loved ones or friends are gone. But how many celebrations did we miss because we didn't feel like going, had competing priorities, or just didn't want to make the effort to go?

I've missed celebrations and later regretted it. I looked at pictures afterward and heard all the stories of the fun, crazy, great time everyone had. I missed out on the memories that were made and later asked myself why, when there was no good reason for not attending. Too many of these missed opportunities led me to think differently about celebrating.

Now, unless I have made previous plans that I wouldn't want to cancel, or something unexpectedly comes up that prevents me from going, I feel it's extremely important to say yes to an invitation. Maybe it's because I am getting older and time with family and friends is more precious than it was when I was younger. Maybe it's because I know that others are getting older and any time you can spend with them is precious and to be cherished. Maybe it's just because I am at a good place in my own life and enjoy celebrating more.

We get invited to special celebrations for a reason. The person requesting that we attend is honoring us with an invitation, and there is a reason why they want us to be there, even though it may be unknown to us. We only get one lifetime to celebrate friends, family, and our own lives as well. The next time you get an invitation, think about it with an open heart. Take the opportunity when it presents itself, and don't be the person missing in the photos. Make magical memories to last a lifetime.

# Stop and Smell
# the Flowers

Do WE EVER JUST TAKE the time to stop and look at what is around us? One day, I was sitting in my car in line waiting for my coffee at our local coffee shop. Suddenly, I looked up from my phone and started to look at the world around me. Not just a passing glance, but a true long look at my surroundings. The more I looked, the more detail I saw, and I began to focus on all the beauty. I saw vibrant green leaves starting to come out on the trees. All the bushes were sprouting buds of new spring flowers. The reds, purples, blues, and just about every color imaginable in nature jumped out. I noticed the sun shining on everything and making it clearer, bolder, and brighter. Why now?

Finally, it came to me. I usually go through my day tied to my cell phone. Even when I have the opportunity to take a few minutes, I can't escape the leash the phone has me on.

Technology has enhanced our lives in many ways. When we tie ourselves to the latest cutting-edge products, we forget to look at what is going on around us and life just drifts by. In that moment, I realized I wasn't having some universal episode that was causing everything to look different. The leaves, the buds, the colors, the sun are always there. What happened was I took the time to put the electronics down and observe life for a change. What a wonderful experience!

How many awe-inspiring things do we miss every day? How often do we get the opportunity to truly admire and appreciate nature, people, and the happenings of a day?

Take five minutes today and walk outside. Leave your phone inside and just be in the moment. Really look at what is around you. See the true colors, feel and smell the fresh air, and take it all in. Be thankful for your surroundings. In doing so, you create a moment that no one else can claim.

# Are You in Love with Being Alive?

I BELIEVE WE OFTEN FORGET to fall in love with being alive. It is difficult to turn on the television, read a Facebook post, or see a news story without some element of sadness or death being a part of what we see. It is all around us, often consumes us, and makes us look at our own mortality. When we are young, we feel infallible, indestructible, and believe that nothing can touch us. As we age and start to lose those around us, the importance of enjoying life becomes even more significant.

Every one of our 1,440 minutes in a day is an opportunity to open our souls and let life in—to enjoy the mundane with the exciting and know that they are each a gift we have been given as we breathe that next breath of life. Acknowledging and working through the strife that comes with that journey only makes us stronger and more aware to make the most of the time we are given.

Why is it so hard to enjoy the simple things of our day? Things like taking that first step out of bed when another day greets us; hugging our loved ones good-bye as we send them off on their day; sitting with that first cup of coffee or tea; or meditating, praying, or just being alone with our thoughts? Throughout the day, we should do the things that make us smile, laugh, cry, and feel emotion. Then when we lay our heads down on our pillows at night, we can give thanks for the gift of another day and all it had to offer.

When we come to the point where we have filled our lives with those things that make us happy, we are armed with the artillery we need to weather the things that make us sad. Feeling alive, present and allowing ourselves to experience life as it was meant to be gives us a reason to fall in love with being alive every day. What will you do with your 1,440 minutes today?

# Happiness

OFTEN, I TELL PEOPLE THAT I hope they have a happy day. What is happiness, though? I can't define happiness because it can be different things to different people. The dictionary defines happiness as "the state of being happy." Well, that's a big help. Generally, happiness is a mental or emotional state of well-being characterized by pleasant emotions. So much for the textbook definitions, but when you get right down to it, what really is happiness?

Many people go through their lives trying to capture a perpetual state of happiness. We often hear, "all I want is to be happy," followed by an expectation that happiness is supposed to rain down upon them 24 hours a day. That expectation itself could be the very reason they never achieve even a brief state of happiness. They have placed so much pressure on themselves to achieve happiness that the pressure prevents them from getting the very thing they are searching for.

Twenty-four-hour happiness isn't realistic because we must deal with what life throws at us every day. However, the more we find things that put us in a state of well-being and cause pleasant emotions, the more we can move the unpleasant emotions to the back seat. Sometimes it is as simple as sitting down and making a list of all the things that truly make you happy and then focusing on doing more of those things. Once you have filled your life with happy, pleasant things, there isn't as much room for unhappiness to seep in. Sounds simple, doesn't it? Putting it into play in real life takes work, but we are rewarded with a greater sense of happiness for having done it.

If you ask me what makes me happy in my life, I could easily rattle off my list to you. Do any of these resonate with you?

- Being with family and savoring every moment of life with them
- Trying a new restaurant with friends and sitting around the table having satisfying, stimulating conversation
- Traveling around the world and learning about other cultures and history
- Playing Mah Jongg with friends and enjoying their camaraderie
- Taking care of and watering the plants around my pool and watching all the new sprouts coming up in the spring
- Prepping cards for delivery to senior communities, knowing the smiles they will bring

… and the list goes on.

Focusing on what makes us happy, no matter what it is, and less on what doesn't, automatically makes us happier people. It's often not about what we want but taking the time to enjoy what we already have. Today, I hope you make your list and find the things that rise to the top. Do them more and put yourself on that journey to a happier you. There is always room for more happiness, and it's often contagious.

# Have Your "30 Minutes
# of Something Wonderful"

IF YOU'VE SEEN THE MOVIE *Steel Magnolias* then you know this quote well. Shelby says this when she finds out she is having a baby despite her struggle with diabetes. She understood the issues she could face, but she made the choice to enjoy one of life's beautiful joys despite the risk. My friend and I were recently talking about this quote, and I happened to think about when opportunities in life are scariest and how not taking advantage of them could leave me with a lifetime of nothing special.

We all live our lives in different ways. Some of us take life by the reins and do everything we can to make it all that it can be. Some of us live life in fear that if we attempt to do something we may fail. Others choose the sheltered approach and decide that a lifetime of nothing special was just their destiny. How unfortunate is that?

Every morning when we wake up, our life can take many different paths and can be full of land mines that we may not even expect. But sometimes there can be something on the other side of those land mines that truly makes our life spectacular. Taking the risk that could result in us having that 30 minutes of something wonderful makes navigating those potential land mines worth it.

When I look back over my life, I find there were many instances where I made decisions that didn't turn out so well. But there were just as many where I took the option that was in front of me, faced the risk, and wound up making my life just that much more special. Using my gut as my guide allows me to live a full and complete life rather than one that really is nothing special.

The next time you are facing the option of that 30 minutes of wonderful or a lifetime of nothing special, I hope you do yourself a favor and choose the wonderful. I always say that we get one chance at life and there are no do-overs. We all deserve fulfilling and amazing lives.

# Me Time

WE ALL EXPERIENCE CRAZY WEEKS from time to time. We often find ourselves looking at our schedule for the day and see that every minute is planned out: work obligations, taking care of family, shopping, errands, cooking, cleaning, etc. If you had to add one more thing, you just don't know where you would fit it in. Is that what happens to you most days? If you were to pull out your schedule and look at it carefully, would you find a space for "me time" on that long list of tasks that need to get done between the time you get up and the time you go to bed?

It amazes me that the last thing that makes any list is a block of time that belongs only to us, for our own personal use, in any way we like. A few moments in the day when we can shut out the outside world and forget about the stress of things we must do. "Me time" is a block of time where we allow ourselves to be selfish with those moments and use them to recharge, regroup, and focus on nothing else but ourselves. What we do with the time is totally up to us. We can use it to take a walk alone, read part of a book, meditate, pray, write, or just sit and be alone with our thoughts.

Running my Bring Smiles to Seniors program along with a full-time job, family, and personal obligations makes me one of the guilty when it comes to avoiding "me time." However, I have learned some techniques that help me to snag the time I need to regroup and recharge. I block out time on my calendar and schedule all work and personal obligations around it. I take 15 minutes out of my day to care for my plants around the pool area, which is something relaxing that I enjoy. I schedule time to meditate and focus on my mind and soul. The important thing is whatever I choose, it's mine, and for that moment of the day I don't belong to anyone else.

We strive to take care of everyone else in our lives, yet we seem to find it difficult to find the time to take care of ourselves. If we aren't "fully charged," how can we expect ourselves to be able to lend a hand to others? If you have gone day after day making sure that the world is taken care of yet haven't taken the time to do the same for yourself, please make it a priority to carve out five minutes today just for you. Expand it to 10 minutes and then 20 minutes and eventually get all the way to an hour. You will find the energy this "me time" gives you to focus on others will be nothing short of miraculous as you learn to focus on yourself.

# The Power of We

SINCE THE BEGINNING OF THE Bring Smile to Seniors program, I've been astounded by the generosity and kindness of people I have never even met. From the first post I made on Facebook asking all my friends to send cards for my grandmother's nursing home, to the boxes of cards I now receive regularly, my faith in humanity has never been greater. When people come together for the common good, a beautiful thing happens and programs such as ours are given life to survive.

I have been in the armed forces, worked tough jobs, had tough bosses, and had struggles in life like most of us. However, I will say that one of the hardest things I have ever done (and most rewarding) is starting a nonprofit. I have an M. B. A., and the process is still daunting. The paperwork needed to establish a 501(c)(3) so that donations are tax deductible, not to mention all the different state filings, are arduous and cumbersome. The administrative side is only half of the effort. You must build supporters, hope for donations, work hard at growing every day, and then just pray it all comes together.

There have been times when I didn't think we would make it. The cards dried up, the decorating avenues became scarce, and we had absolutely no money to do anything. In the back of my head I kept hearing my grandmother say the same thing she told me over and over, "Never start a job unless you are going to finish it, and never do it unless you are going to do it right." Most importantly, all along the way I never stopped believing in the people who were a part of our journey. At every point when things seemed dire, a new connection was made that kept us alive.

We continue to grow because of every card artist, decorator, teacher, student, principal, civic group leader, friend, family member, corporate partner, and individual who supports the Bring Smiles to Seniors program. These individuals believe in our cause, our need, and the positive effect we can have on the aging population.

Together, we've created this safe positive place for individuals to visit and participate. On all our social media sites, you see people supporting each other and providing words of encouragement and positive messages. We will continue to innovate and work to expand our reach as far as we can take it. All of that will be possible because of the POWER of WE.

# Outside Our
# Comfort Zone

SOMETIMES WE LIVE OUR LIVES in a bubble or a room with four walls. The edge of the bubble or one of those walls becomes the extent that we discover life. Just outside those confined areas are unexplored places, people we haven't met, adventures we haven't had, and a world of possibilities we may never know.

When I was in the Air Force, I was sent to Adana, Turkey on my first assignment. I was fresh out of boot camp and tech school. At 19, I was sent halfway across the world to a land I had to find on a map. Upon my arrival, I was placed in a small room in one of the dorms on the base. I was a little reluctant to leave the base as Turkey was under martial law at the time, and men with machine guns were everywhere. I talked to people who had never stepped foot off the base in the two years they had been there for fear of what was outside the gates. This situation presented me with a choice. I could either follow in others' footsteps and stay inside where I knew it was safe, or I could take a chance and venture out and see what the outside world was like.

I grew up in a small town where we didn't lock our doors at night. Everyone knew everyone else. The most natural thing for me to do was to play it safe, confine myself to the base, serve out my assignment, and get back to the States. However, something inside of me, along with a little help from the Air Force, prompted me to make a different decision.

Due to a dorm shortage, the Air Force offered to pay people to live off base, and this 19-year-old got an apartment above a shop in the local village and promptly moved in. It turned out to be one of the most amazing decisions of my life. I immersed myself in the culture and met new and interesting people. I started to learn the Turkish language. I ate Turkish food, got invited to families' homes, and learned about the Turkish culture and people. I was awed by their amazing respect for the elderly. When visiting a Turkish home, the most senior member of the family always sits nearest the door. That way, in case of an emergency, they are the first to safety. When sitting, you don't sit with your legs crossed where the soles of your feet are showing. It's considered disrespectful to your elders. The list goes on.

Because I chose to get out of the bubble and leave the four walls, I had experiences that most 19-year-olds never get. By following my instincts, I made friends that I have had for over 30 years and still see today. I also learned a valuable lesson. Life can be scary, but by locking ourselves within our comfort zone, we take a chance that we are going to miss all the incredible experiences life has to offer.

If you find yourself confined to your bubble or your four walls, you don't have to start big to get out and discover the beauty that life has to offer. Pick one small thing that you always wanted to do, see, or experience. Take just one step outside your comfort zone, and, before you know it, your small steps will become big steps. Soon, you will be running. We only get one chance. Live life, enjoy life, and be yourself. Explore the outside of your cocoon and see just how exciting it can be.

# Grandma Lola Mae:
# Never Start a Job Unless…

ONE OF THE MOST PRECIOUS THINGS that grandparents and parents pass on to their children are those little pearls of wisdom that they learned in their lives that guide and direct ours. We may not see or agree with the wisdom at the time, but inevitably we face a situation where a recollection of that pearl is exactly what we need to get us through. An experience in high school showed me just how valuable that wisdom can be.

When I was growing up, my grandmother got me a job at Ben Franklin, the local five-and-dime store. The owner asked my grandmother if I would come to work for him. I worked there for the last three years of high school until I went off to college. Although a fair man, he was definitely a taskmaster. He was often brash, expected perfection, and added a lot of unneeded stress to the position. There were many times when I would go home crying, and I just wanted to quit. When I would do this, I was always met with the same comment from my grandmother. "You can't quit," she would say. My grandmother would tell me to buck up and do my best.

My grandmother also reminded me that throughout your life, you are going to work for people who may not be easy to work for, and it will be impossible for you to walk away every time you aren't happy. She also shared these words that have resonated with me my whole life: "Never start a job unless you are going to finish it, and never do a job unless you are going to do it right." Those words have served me well and helped me get through many situations in life, despite sometimes difficult circumstances.

Although we may not absorb those pearls of wisdom when they are given, we eventually learn that there are times when our elders really do know best. We can learn from their experience, if we only take the time to truly listen.

# Grandma Lola Mae:
# Ringing the Bell

M Y GRANDMOTHER WAS A STRONG WOMAN. She had to be, raising three children on her own in the 1940s after my grandfather left. She would often tell me stories of the hard times and how difficult it was to make sure there was food on the table and clothes on her children's backs. She wasn't afraid of the hard work needed to make that happen. She worked in a canning plant and a meat packing plant for years until she landed a job at the Florida School for Boys where she worked for over 40 years. Until the time she retired, she was the warehouse manager on campus, and it was normal for me to go see her after school and find her driving the forklift, moving pallets around. She kept meticulous books and records, and her warehouse was spotless. During this time, she had what she needed to care for herself, but the earlier days caring for her children weren't so easy.

In the early years of her children's lives, she often said she would not have been able to put food on the table had it not been for the help she got from the Salvation Army. However, she would also say that with that help came responsibility. Because of her need to honor them, for most of her life, until she no longer could do so, you would always find her in front of a store with a bell in her hand and a kettle by her side collecting donations during the holidays.

With her children grown and her newfound self-sufficiency, she no longer needed the Salvation Army, but she knew they needed her, and she never forgot that.

You see, her strength came not only from her religious beliefs—and she was definitely a woman of God—it came from her ingrained belief that no matter how little you had, you always gave back in thanks for what you were given. I really believe that it was her struggle to survive that gave her the will and the passion to take care of others later in her life, a gift she so generously passed on to me.

When she passed several years ago, we were going through old photos to make a collage for her service. I came upon many pictures that showed her strength and vitality. They also showed a woman ready to take on life no matter what was thrown at her. And take on life she did. There is no doubt in my mind that—up in heaven—she is still driving forklifts, keeping spotless warehouses, and ringing those bells.

# Grandma Lola Mae:
# The Cake

A NYONE WHO KNEW MY GRANDMOTHER knew that she made the best pound cake on the planet. She had her own special recipe. It was a delicious lemon pound cake with a crunchy top. Those who had the pleasure of savoring a piece of this cake had their own way of eating it. Some would eat the bottom first and save the top for last. Others would warm it and put a little butter on it (as if it didn't have enough butter already). Others would freeze it and save it for another day to toast. No matter your choice, every bite contained a little bit of her love that made it even more special.

As long as I can remember, my Grandma would bake cakes and take them to the sick and the elderly and to places all over town. When she would go to the bank, she would put a slice in the teller's drawer with her deposit. When she would go to the doctor, she would take an entire cake for the staff. We came from a small town, and everywhere she went everyone knew about Grandma Lola Mae's pound cake. It was not unusual for her to make three to five cakes in a day. She had a lot of people to serve.

My grandmother lived with my mom and dad for many years until she spent her last three years in a nursing home due to her dementia. Her cake baking got to the point where my parents were buying flour and sugar for her in 25-pound bags and eggs by the dozens. She had her own special way of cutting out circles from cardboard boxes for the bases of the cakes. She knew exactly when to wrap the cakes after cooling to make sure they stayed soft and delicious when they were delivered. Anyone who knew her knew about and wanted her cake.

Because her cakes were part of the very essence of who she was, one of the hardest moments for me was when her dementia got to the point where she could no longer bake. The cakes no longer came out perfect because there was too much flour, or too much sugar, or she had forgotten the eggs or had not remembered that they were in the oven at all. Her memory faded until she reached the point where she was no longer able to bake at all. Fortunately, my mom has mastered my grandmother's techniques, and her legacy lives on.

When I think back on all the smiles she created with those cakes, the sick she made feel better, the lonely she brought some warmth to, and the pure joy that she brought to so many, it makes my heart full. These weren't just cakes. These were Grandma Lola Mae's pound cakes! They are one of the things I miss about her most of all. Sometimes, if I close my eyes and imagine, I can still smell them baking in the oven and wonder if I can sneak a piece before she has a chance to notice.

# Grandma Lola Mae:
# The Jar

WHEN I WAS A KID, I SPENT a lot of time with my grandmother. She lived alone and I would often stay over at her house and go to school straight from there. I loved my sleepovers, except for the fact that she always made me eat oatmeal in the morning before I went to school. I hated oatmeal, but she told me it would keep me full and make me strong, so I obliged. In full disclosure, I love oatmeal today.

We lived in a small town, and I had a paper route delivering the local newspaper. When I would return from my route, we would sit down and count out the change I had in my pocket from the money I had made along the way. Up on the shelf, she would keep a Mason jar. My grandmother would take down the jar, and half of what I made would go in the jar and the other half I could spend however I wanted. We did this repeatedly during the time I continued my paper route. When I asked her why we were doing this, she told me how she struggled through her life, that she wanted me to go to college, and she wanted to make sure that I always had something. She told me that as long as there was money in the jar, I would never be broke. I sort of understood it at the time, but later in life I would learn what it meant.

As I went through life, that jar became a symbol of so many things for me. I met people whose jar was empty that I could help fill a little. I encountered people whose emotional jar was empty and I could help nourish them. Most of all, I revered the fact that it meant so much to my grandmother to see that my jar was never empty and that I honored her by making sure that it never was. I also honored her dream and went on to finish college, eventually earning an MBA.

For years, I kept a $50 bill folded and tucked in my wallet so that I would never be out of money, even when times were bleak. I still have a jar, no longer a Mason jar, but an electronic one that reminds me of the lesson she taught. To this day, when I see a Mason jar I think of my grandmother and smile. I remember how important it is for your jar never to be empty and how equally important it is to make sure that other people's jars are not empty as well.

# Grandma Lola Mae:
# The Trip

M Y GRANDMOTHER WORKED FOR a school for wayward boys for 40 years. Although she held various positions during her tenure there, I think the one thing that she was most proud of was her last job as warehouse manager. She ran a meticulous warehouse that was responsible for an inventory of all the supplies that came in and went out of the campus. Those who knew her knew that she was not afraid of hard work. It was in her DNA, and she lived her life that way. Any task she asked her employees to do, she did herself. It didn't matter if it was bookkeeping, cleaning, rearranging or even driving the forklift. You could eat off the floor in her warehouse, and she demanded excellence not only from her employees but from herself.

When she finally decided to retire, there were a lot of sad people on the campus. They got together and threw her a party. In addition, they collected money and gave her a trip to the Bahamas for two. I was the lucky recipient of the second slot on the trip, and Grandma and I set off to celebrate her retirement. Now most people would think that going on vacation with your grandmother wouldn't exactly be ideal. But I will tell you that for me it was the trip of a lifetime. Not only did I get to experience another place, I got to experience it through her eyes, and that made it special and created memories that have lasted a lifetime.

We experienced the local culture, shopped in the local shops, and dined on the local food. But one experience stood out from all the rest. In our hotel, a Las Vegas-style show was part of our trip package. As the curtain opened and the set was revealed, we were excited to see the glitz and glamour of it all. As the show started, the showgirls paraded out on the stage, and I quickly noticed that they were topless. I was completely horrified. I couldn't even look at my grandmother. But when I finally did, she was stoic with no expression at all on her face. I crouched down on my seat and held my breath and we made it through. After the show, we shared not a word of what we had just seen, and I sure wasn't going to bring it up.

The point of the story is this. As life goes by, we are presented with chances to create memories with those we love. It is so important to take advantage of those opportunities. Doing so gives us a book full of wonderful memories that stay with us long after our loved one is gone. Failing to do so creates missed opportunities that we don't get a second chance to experience. When I was visiting my grandmother in the last days of her life, I didn't see the small frail woman who was sitting in the wheelchair in front of me. I saw the vibrant strong woman who walked on the beach with me in the Bahamas, who took me for a ride on the forklift in her warehouse, and who remained calm and stoic while I was horrified during the show. I knew that although she didn't remember me outwardly, somewhere deep inside we were still walking on the beach in the Bahamas together.

# Grandma Lola Mae:
# I'm There

WE OFTEN HEAR FROM TEACHERS about some parents' lack of involvement in their children's lives. This includes classes where many students no longer have both parents involved, parent-teacher nights where two to three parents show up, or emails that go unanswered when there are critical situations that need to be addressed.

Fortunately, I was not one of those children. I was involved in many activities growing up. I was a member of the band since middle school, participated in speech and oratorical contests, was a member of 4-H, active in student government, and a member of drama class, to name a few. I cannot remember a single event where I would look out in the audience and not find my grandmother and mother sitting there. They worked their schedules around mine, and they never said they were too busy or simply could not attend. Because they were always there, I think I took it for granted that it was just the norm.

I remember one instance where I had been selected to participate in the American Legion oratorical contest. One of the requirements was that I had to deliver a speech, not from paper but from memory. I was having difficulty memorizing the speech, and my grandmother sat with me and had me read it and recite it over and over. When she and I would go on our outings, she would even have me practice it with the people we were visiting. Just when I thought I could not study it anymore, she would have me recite it again. One night, it just clicked, and I went on to win local, district, and regional contests and placed second in the state. I remember one of our local members came over to me after the contest was over and told me how I had let them down by not winning. True to form, my grandmother and mother stepped in, delivered a few choice words of their own, and let him know just how proud they were of my accomplishment. As he sheepishly wandered off, they turned what could have made me feel like a failure into a proud moment that still resonates with me today.

We sometimes forget that our actions have a lasting impact on how our children develop and feel about themselves. Early lessons give them a sense of confidence and purpose and set them on a path that will shape them later in life. Because my grandmother and mother were always there, I had the protection that I needed to avoid the feelings of failure that could have ensued.

This was just one of many experiences that explains why I have been so passionate about having children involved in the Bring Smiles to Seniors program. I want them to learn early on the importance that seniors continue to play in our lives and why it is so necessary for us to remember and appreciate the fact that they were there for us. The lessons I learned early on made me the man I am today. Elders in our lives have amazing guidance to give if we just take the time to listen. As children, we think we know it all. We don't, and that is a lesson we sometimes learn too late.

# Grandma Lola Mae:
# The Delivery

Bring Smiles to Seniors was started because of my grandmother, and it will live on in her memory. Because it was started in the last year of her life, I often wondered if she ever really knew that I had done it. I told her about it and described it to her, but the mute reaction that she had to my description left me wondering if she truly knew.

On one of my visits to her, my friend Linda, who has been with the Bring Smiles to Seniors program from the beginning, accompanied me on my visit to her senior community in Okeechobee, Florida. We had decided to do a card delivery on this visit and hand out cards to the residents there. However, when we arrived and found my grandmother bright and alert that day, we came up with a much different plan that turned out to be one of the best decisions we could make.

Usually, when we go into communities, we hand-deliver the cards to the residents one by one. We chat with them and tell them to have a wonderful day. We see the smiles on their faces when they open a card from a stranger. Sometimes they can't see well enough to read the card, and we read it to them out loud and watch the brightness that comes across their faces. On this visit, we got the idea to have Grandma do the deliveries herself. So, we loaded her up with cards, pushed her through the aisles in her wheelchair, and began an amazing journey with her.

Helping people was at the very core of my grandmother's beliefs. Even in the late stage of her life that belief never left her. The smile on her face as she handed the cards to the residents gave me the answer I was looking for. She knew what we were doing. Not only did she know, she was a part of it. She laughed, she smiled, and you could tell by the look on her face that she was in her element as she handed each resident their card. On this day she wasn't a dementia patient in a nursing home, she was the grandmother I always knew. I was reminded of the importance of treating her that way.

It is so important when dealing with dementia and Alzheimer's patients not to forget that they are still people. Treat them like they understand and give them a reason to be present. This moment was not only heartwarming and fulfilling for us, it gave my grandmother an hour of normalcy. At that point in time, she was who she had always been when she was at her best. From Grandma's smile with the bag of cards in her lap at the beginning of the delivery to the high five with Linda when the delivery was finished, every moment was filled with a sense of accomplishment.

Over the years in the Bring Smiles to Seniors program, we've experienced special moments that will stay with us a lifetime. But this visit will always be dearest to me because it was then that I knew that Grandma was aware of the program and what we were doing. I believe in all my heart that she understood and at that very moment she infused Bring Smiles to Seniors with the lifeblood that will keep it going for many years to come.

If you encounter a person with dementia or Alzheimer's this week, give them a hug and let them know they are loved. Treat them as if they are still there and remind them that they matter.

# Grandma Lola Mae: The Social Hall

IF YOU BUILD IT, THEY WILL COME" is a line from the charming 1989 movie *Field of Dreams*. The line caught on and became part of American conversation. It's a movie about a man who resolves a lifelong internal conflict with his father by building a baseball field in the middle of an Iowa cornfield, and people did come to watch baseball. Sometimes this saying gets played out in real life with similar heartwarming results.

Such is the case with the First United Methodist Church in Okeechobee, Florida. My grandmother was a member of the First United Methodist Church since she moved to Okeechobee in the 1940s from Miami. My mom and dad were married there, and my brother and I were baptized and attended church there until we moved away. Grandma always made sure we were at Wednesday evening service, Sunday school, and Sunday morning/evening services. We were also a part of the church youth group. The church had no social facilities, and the parishioners decided to add an extension to the existing building that would become the social hall for church gatherings.

The church called on people with expertise in carpentry, electrical, and construction to help build this new wing. Can you guess who was the first one to raise her hand? Every day after work and on Saturdays (my grandmother was a strict believer that you didn't work on Sunday), my grandmother was there. She had a tool belt around her waist and a hammer in her hand, and she was climbing ladders alongside the men working on the building. When they were tired at night and ready to quit for the day, she would urge them to stay a little longer. When they were gone, you could go down to the building and find her there alone finishing up any last-minute tasks or cleaning up from the day's work, using up her last bit of energy. She would then get up in the morning, go to her job managing the warehouse and was right back out there again in the evening.

Some women watched in awe and others were appalled that she would insert herself in "men's work," but she didn't care. Grandma never lived her life caring what others thought. She lived it knowing that she was secure in who she was and in her faith. The hall still stands today as a living testament to her and others who made it a reality.

Several years ago, we used the hall for the repast after her funeral service. As I sat there having my meal, I could still feel her presence and looked around in awe at what she had been a part of. Sometimes people try to put us in boxes where they think we should be. But if we open those boxes and let our true selves come out, the things we can accomplish in the world are amazing.

The next time you are facing a challenge, think about Grandma Lola Mae on the ladder with her hammer. Dig deep, and maybe you will find the inner strength to accomplish what you thought was impossible.

# Grandma Lola Mae: The Hitchhiker

IT WAS A DIFFERENT WORLD growing up as a boy in the 60s and 70s. I spent a lot of time on the road with my grandmother. We went out of town visiting family and friends, which often took us not only all over Florida but to all the states between Florida and Pennsylvania and one special trip to Canada.

Back in those days, there were a lot of hitchhikers. Most of the time, they were military men trying to get from one town to another. Some had just come back from the war; others were men who just needed to get somewhere. No matter where we went, we never passed a hitchhiker without stopping to offer them a ride—never. This was a little unnerving for me and even more unnerving for my mother, but my grandmother didn't care. Helping people was in her DNA, and if she saw someone in need, she helped. Granted, in those days we didn't have the heightened concerns that exist today.

There was an instance that stands out for me that taught me a lesson about the power of generosity. On one of our trips to south Florida, we passed a broken-down truck on the side of the road. It was a delivery truck, and the man standing by the truck trying to get a ride seemed to be in great despair. As always, we pulled up alongside the truck and Grandma spoke to the man to see what help she could offer. He said he needed a part for the truck, but we were

10 miles from the nearest town. Grandma insisted that we take him into town to get the part he needed, and off we went. Of course, we waited, and as soon as the part was secured, we took the man back to his truck. But did we just drop him off and go on our way? No, Grandma—of course—helped him fix the truck.

When he was done, he went to the back of the truck and took out a little box and handed it to me to say thank you. You see, this was no ordinary truck. The reason he was in such despair was that he was hauling packaged food that the astronauts used on their space flights. That was exactly what was in the box he gave to me. To this day, I wish I saved it. But I was hungry, so, of course, I ate it! Because of his kind gesture, I also learned a lesson of compassion and caring that resonates with me all these years later.

A small act of kindness is often rewarded with a corresponding act of kindness, even when it isn't expected. Most likely today one would never think of picking up a hitchhiker on the side of the road. The world is a lot different and a lot scarier than in those days. My guess is, though, that if there is any chance there are cars in heaven, Grandma's door is still wide open to anyone she passes who needs a ride.

# Grandma Lola Mae: The Toothache

WHEN I WAS IN HIGH SCHOOL, I was involved in speech and debate. As part of those activities, I often participated in oratorical contests that were sponsored by the American Legion. One of the contest requirements was that the student had to deliver both a memorized speech and an extemporaneous speech based on a series of topics. For me, memorization was the hardest part, as the speeches were quite lengthy. I had a way to help me practice. When my grandmother and I would visit friends and shut-ins around town, she would have me recite the speech for them. She knew the more exposure and opportunity I had to recite and repeat the speeches, the more the words would sink in and the memorization would finally occur. While most people were gracious and gladly sat through my speech, I am sure there were some who probably got a little tired of listening to me, but they politely indulged me.

One weekend stands out for me. I was staying at my grandmother's house, and she had set aside time for us to keep working on memorization. Unfortunately, I also had a massive toothache, which was greatly affecting my concentration, and all I wanted to do was quit and surrender to the pain. There were no dentists working on the weekend, and I was going to have to endure until we could get to one on Monday.

The contest was two weeks away and I wasn't feeling confident, so my grandmother insisted that continued practice was important and that I would need to cope with my pain. She reminded me that there would be times in my life when situations would come up that would not be helpful to what I was trying to accomplish. She said there may be times when I would be dealing with pain, raw emotions, uncomfortable circumstances, or other outside influences that would keep me from focusing on my intended goal. She suggested that it was in those times that I would need to dig deep to find the inner strength to pull me through. I was never to take my eyes off the ultimate objective. At the time, I didn't understand how any of that would make my tooth feel any better. However, as I look back at that moment, I now see that it was the catalyst for how I would deal with similar situations in the future.

That year, I went on to win the oratorical contest at the local, district, and regional levels and came in second at state finals. I was successful because I found the will to persevere. Today, when things seem to be dire, I go back to that moment and my conversation with my grandmother. I dig a little deeper to find the inner strength to get through whatever I may be facing.

Growing up, we often fail to see that parents and grandparents usually know best. It is only later in life that we discover that to be true. Seniors have a wealth of information to help guide and shape us if only we would listen. Many times, we do not listen, only to later discover that we wish we had.

# Thankful For

MANY OF OUR LIVES PROVIDE us with so much that it is important to have an ongoing practice where we pick something that we are thankful for and focus on it. For me, this usually happens during my "thankful Thursdays." Many times, my focus is on my family and the support they provided my brother and me throughout our childhood. One day, I concentrated on our family's gifts of provision, courteousness, compassion, and love.

My parents and grandmother both worked when my brother and I were children. They had to so they could survive and provide. I can't count the times they went without so that my brother and I could have. My mom made her own clothes so that my brother and I could have store-bought ones. My dad labored at the county road department. My grandmother worked in the boys' school warehouse and helped the family when she could. They did all of this to ensure that my brother and I had the kind of childhood my parents wanted for us.

Our family's commitment to provide for us came with the responsibility to live a good and courteous life. We were taught right from wrong early on. We lived in the South so we always—*always*—replied with "yes, ma'am" and "yes, sir." We participated in school and civic activities as much as we wanted, but we were also required to attend church Wednesday night, Sunday morning, and Sunday evening. Through it all, we were allowed to be who we were and were never pressured to be what we weren't.

The best gift our parents and grandmother gave us was our compassion for others and an innate need and desire to give back. Through charitable work, visiting the sick and elderly, and civic responsibilities, they instilled in us a sense of selflessness that would carry through our entire lives. I believe their teachings set us both on the path to become the people we are just by being the parents and grandparent they were supposed to be.

As children, we can take many paths—some great, some not as good. Having been fortunate enough to have the love and support of a family like ours made taking the right path easy. Sometimes that is all children need—parents who are there, provide the moral guidance, let them be who they are, and give them the tools and foundations to build the life you hope for them. I am grateful for and thank my mom, Alice, dad, Kenneth, and Grandma Lola Mae for making that path for us. Through my work with Bring Smiles to Seniors and my brother's work with his charity helping service members with PTSD, we are striving to leave the world a little better off than we found it.

# Remember to Ask

I LOVE SPENDING WEEKENDS WITH MY mom and dad. The quality time I get with them gives me time to think. On a recent visit I was reminded of how a simple request for a recipe led to a reminder to seek knowledge from those around us while the opportunity is still available.

While we were preparing for our family trip to North Carolina for my dad's 80th birthday, my mom called and asked me if I had my grandmother's baked bean recipe. I searched, but it appeared that I also did not have it. Grandma had passed several years before, and I suddenly realized that if neither of us could find it, it was lost forever.

On my visit, my parents and I were talking about the fact that, as we age, many of the people we would like to ask about our family history are now gone and with them their knowledge. In some cases, they don't even have to be gone. They could be still alive but suffering from dementia, Alzheimer's, or other ailments that rob them of their memories. Those who have family members who are fighting these debilitating diseases know all too well how lucky people are when they have family members still around to answer their questions. Fortunately, for many of us there is still the opportunity to learn what we want to know. The question is whether we take the time to sit down with these individuals and ask.

Think about some of your recent family visits. Are they spent exchanging the normal pleasantries and then you just do what you need to do to get through it so you can go on with your own life? Or, do you take the time to have a conversation and learn all there is to know about them, your history, and their lives before you can no longer do that? By having that conversation with my parents on this visit, I learned about relatives I never knew, stories about how my parents met, and more about what life was like for them when they were growing up.

For many people, things have happened that have estranged them from their family members, the people they were once closest to. Often, there is good reason why those chasms have been created. However, at some point we should ask ourselves if it is worth waiting, taking the chance that they will no longer be there to repair what we might not think repairable. We can only do that when it is right for us.

Do you have a little family history that you want to know? It is often only a phone call or a visit away. Make the effort to have the conversation and remember to ask. Sometimes you will learn things that you never even knew that can be used to enrich your own life. I am thankful that I still have that opportunity and plan to ask all the questions I can, while I can.

# Paving the Way
# for Us

ONE OF THE GOALS OF THE Bring Smiles to Seniors program is to make sure that people who paved the way for us are remembered and reminded that they are loved and cared for. Honoring them for the sacrifices they made so we would have a better life should be a part of our everyday routine.

History has shown us many generations over the years. Each generation travels through life hoping to leave the world a better place for future generations. Many people have children, grandchildren, nieces, and nephews. They go through life hoping that they can make the world better for their families. Some generations do a great job, some not so great. But, in most cases, people in each generation work to create a bright future for those who come after them. Their contributions were numerous.

Some people worked multiple jobs so their families could eat. Some served in the armed forces to protect our freedom. Some created cures for debilitating diseases and others made discoveries that changed the way we live. Mothers took care of homes and children, sometimes while working regular jobs. Fathers took care of their families and provided so their families could have a good life.

Each generation passes laws, makes advancements, and develops new technologies. This paves the way for future generations.

When those individuals grow older, it's the responsibility of younger people to respect them and remember their sacrifices. We need to let older folks know that they are cared for, loved, and will be remembered when they pass on. They should leave this life knowing we appreciate what they did and that we acknowledge the love they gave us.

Posthumous love serves no purpose. So, take a moment and remind that special someone who paved the way for you how much they mean to you. You will both benefit from your gratitude.

# Doing Without
# So We Could Have

SOMETIMES YOU DON'T TRULY understand the sacrifices that your parents made so that you could have a better life until much later. I think about the selflessness my parents showed so we did not have to go without all the time.

When I grew up, my mom and dad worked to make sure the family was taken care of. We didn't have a lot of money, but they managed to put a roof over our heads and food in our stomachs. As kids, we didn't think this was anything out of the ordinary. It was just supposed to happen. As we got older and started to take care of ourselves, it became apparent that it was so much more than we knew.

My mom never bought new clothes for herself and made her own clothes so my brother and I could have new clothes for school. I think it was after we graduated school that she finally started buying store-bought clothes. At Christmastime, Mom and Dad went out of their way to make sure that at least some of the things we had asked for wound up under the tree. And they often did without so that we had the money to do the things that we wanted to do in school.

I have a strong childhood memory that I carry with me to this day about this subject. My mom and I were in the store. Refrigerated rolled cookies had just come on the market. I had taken a roll off the cooler shelf and put it into our shopping cart without my mom noticing. She finally spotted it and told me to put it back as there were items we needed more. I am not sure if it was her desire for me to have it or the hurt look on my face but before the shopping trip was over, she went back and took the refrigerated cookie roll off the shelf and said we were getting it. She went without something that she needed so that I could have that cookie dough. That was just one experience of many.

I have never forgotten my parents' moments of sacrifice and love and that is why today I go out of my way to do for my parents for all the years that they did for me. We must appreciate the sacrifices that our parents made for us. Making sure children are taken care of is an unspoken oath they take when they decide to have children. Finding a balance in meeting a child's needs while teaching them responsibility by not giving them everything they want is an art that we could use just a little more of today. Realizing our parents did without so that we could have and being thankful for it makes us better people.

# A Lesson Learned

As we go through life, there are lessons we learn that may seem awful at the time but wind up being points in our life that set us on a better path than we might have otherwise chosen. One such lesson happened for me when I was young, and I am so thankful for the actions that my parents took at the time to make it right.

Before I reached my teens, I always wanted to be a server in a restaurant. Had I known how hard a server's job is, as I learned later in life, I might have thought differently. As a result, I thought that it would be really cool to set up a play restaurant in the house while my parents were at work and practice with my brother and cousins. However, to accomplish this I was missing a very important item that was used back in those days in restaurants. Remember when they used to take orders on paper order books and sent those off to the kitchen for the order to be made? Well, I needed one of those. The only problem was I had no money. What was I to do?

We had a five-and-dime in the middle of town that I knew had them. On my next visit with my mom and grandmother, I slipped away from them and managed to put one of the booklets in my pants without anyone knowing. Success! I could now open my pretend restaurant. However, guilt unexpectedly started creeping up on me. I knew what I had done was wrong. Eventually it got the best of me and I wound up telling my parents what I did. What do you think they did? After a good scolding, they marched me right down to the five-and-dime and made me tell the store owner what I had done, apologize and made me pay for the book. But that wasn't the end of it. As with many stories, this one has a twist.

In my sophomore year of high school, I was working at a bakery and my grandmother was in the five-and-dime one day, and the owner came up to her and asked if I would be interested in coming to work for him. He remembered what had happened all those years ago and thought I had done an admirable thing. I quickly accepted and worked for him until I graduated high school and went off to college.

Had my actions gone unchecked, that experience may have had a very different effect on my life. Looking back, I am so thankful to my family for caring enough to make me do the right thing. The sense of accountability and responsibility that I was taught by this event served me well throughout my life.

# We Do What
# We Have to Do

IN OUR SOCIETY, WE'RE PAYING a lot of attention to the fact that our senior population is growing much larger as baby boomers become increasingly older. Because I am a baby boomer, I am keenly aware of the aging of my generation. Some baby boomers are facing the added responsibility of becoming caregivers for their parents, especially as we continue to deal with rising rates of Alzheimer's, dementia, and other debilitating diseases.

There is so much time spent on caring for those with these diseases that we lose sight of the caregivers. Anyone who hasn't experienced that responsibility firsthand or had a parent or friend who has had to shoulder that responsibility may not understand the toll it takes on the caregiver.

My grandmother lived with my parents for more than 30 years. She developed dementia in the last five years of her life. She started showing signs much earlier, we just didn't recognize them. My mom was determined to take care of her until the end. When she kept trying to run away, my mom slept on the floor at the foot of her bed every night to make sure she was safe. My mom was with my grandmother constantly to make sure that she had the right care. When she became combative and a danger to herself and others, the family had to make a decision every family dreads: put her into

RON TYSON: MORNINGS WITH RON

nursing care. Even then, my mom and dad were at the nursing facility every day, making sure she was clean and had a decorated room and all the comforts of home. My mom always said, "We do what we have to do."

A year and a half after my grandmother passed, the family would do it all over again for my mom's younger brother. Her brother passed very quickly from dementia when he was nearing 70. He was not in a community close to home, so trips out of town were added to the routine. Once again, my mom said, "We do what we have to do".

I have friends who were once available to go out to dinner on a moment's notice. Now they work their regular jobs and spend evenings and weekends taking care of an elderly parent. I spent seven years of my relationship alone every other weekend so that my significant other could take care of a father with Parkinson's so the sister could get a break from taking care of him all week. We did that because "We do what we have to do."

Caregivers are unsung heroes in these situations. They show immeasurable devotion and love. The pieces of their life they sacrifice to care for others and the selflessness they exhibit are beautiful things in life that are rarely celebrated. They often run themselves into the ground, sometimes to the detriment of their own health to ensure another's well-being.

People may look up to sports stars, movie stars, or others in the entertainment world as their heroes. Caregivers are my heroes. These are the people who give so that others can have. These are the people who show true love, compassion, and dedication even though they are dealt a hand that they didn't ask for. These are the people who "do what we have to do," and we should honor them for showing us what caring is all about.

# Connections for Life

PEOPLE ARE CONSTANTLY COMING and going in and out of our lives. While we meet people who we often never see again, we meet others who we don't see for a long time who somehow find their way back into our lives. Then, there are those people who come into our lives and stay there forever.

I am very fortunate and count my blessings every day that I have a close group of friends. They've been my friends for 20-plus years. It's pretty rare that a group of people could stay together for so long, and I try to let them know how much I appreciate them in every way that I can. We can never take friends for granted. They are only on loan to us for this lifetime, and we should make every minute count.

I always tell my good friend Linda that people don't come into our lives by chance, they come into our lives because they were meant to be there. Those lifelong connections are important to the stability of our lives. But sometimes people choose quantity over quality and, in doing so, miss out on more intimate connections with friends. They have so many "friends" that there isn't enough time to interact with any one person.

My philosophy on nurturing and taking care of these life connections is that the old saying "the more the merrier" doesn't work. I have seen people stretched so thin that getting any time with them takes months. In the end, it's hardly worth the effort. At the same time, there are people you may not see for years who, when you do meet up again, it seems like time has never passed and you pick up right where you left off. Those are the true friends who are meant to be in our lives.

Perhaps it's time to make a reconnection with those people who have come into your life with whom you may have fallen out of touch. Maybe you need to let certain people in your life know how important they are to you. There may even be those who you just want to reach out to today and say hello. Do it! Make the time. We only get one life to enjoy those with whom we have been bestowed the blessing of a life connection. Growing those friendships is a two-way street, and both parties are responsible to keep it going. Nurturing is an important part of growing, and it's only with that effort that friendships become true life connections.

# Ruby

I OFTEN THINK BACK TO MY DAYS when I was in the Air Force and especially about a woman who became one of the most important people in my life. I served for four years at Incirlik Air Base in Adana, Turkey and the remainder of my time at MacDill AFB in Tampa. While at MacDill, I worked in the base hospital. Every day, I would go to the hospital cafeteria for lunch and there was an African-American lady who worked behind the counter who would always catch my eye. I was in my early 20s, and she was about 30 years older than me. Every time I went through the line, she greeted me with her amazing smile and always said something to make me laugh.

One day, we started talking about a sport played in Florida called jai alai. We both had an interest in it and decided that we were going to try it out. I picked her up, and we set out on our adventure. After several of these outings, Ruby became one of the best friends of my life. Her laugh was infectious and her love of life—despite her lack of material possessions—was amazing. We often went to dinner together. Over the years, I also took her to the Bahamas, Las Vegas, and to my childhood home to Okeechobee where she became good friends with my grandmother. She had a love for fishing and bowling, and the simplest of things would bring joy to her life.

Although I didn't have much money then, I was determined that she was going to have things to make her life a little better. We were friends in the South in the early 80s. You can imagine the stares from people when they saw this twentysomething white man hanging out and enjoying life with a black woman in her fifties.

Growing up, I spent a lot of time with my grandmother, so being with Ruby, someone much older, was nothing out of the ordinary for me. Ruby and I never lost touch when I moved from Tampa, and she was so thrilled when I moved back in 2012. Unfortunately, about three years after I returned, Ruby passed away. I had the honor of being asked to deliver the eulogy at her funeral, which I did proudly.

My friendship with Ruby taught me a valuable lesson. When we believe that age, race, and gender have no bearing on our ability to have a friendship, we can have rich relationships with a sense of respect that stays with us throughout our lives. True friendships are not constrained by ethnic or socioeconomic boundaries. True friendships come from like-minded people who share a sense of compassion and caring for each other, simply because of who they are. I miss Ruby, but I know that she is in heaven looking down on me every day. Everyone should have someone in their life who brings as much joy as Ruby did for me.

# A Mother's
# Special Love

I WANT TO SHARE WITH YOU a story about a person who has been in my life for many years. I've always looked up to how she lives her life as a mother. She is someone who shows strength and resolve while facing her responsibilities. Because of her circumstances, this takes extra effort beyond the normal mothering requirements. This woman meets her responsibilities head on, and acts on them in a way that creates a special bond between her and her daughter that some mothers wish they had.

When you're an expectant mother, you experience lots of excitement as you get ready for the day you will meet your child for the first time. As much as you think you are ready for that moment, nothing can prepare you for the birth of a Down syndrome child and the painstaking extra care and surgeries the child needs. There are many ways people can deal with this situation. How they do so defines the kind of parent they are and will be.

If you have never had the wonderful opportunity of meeting a Down syndrome child, you are missing out. They truly are the gift that keeps on giving. They are filled with immeasurable love and compassion. But caring for them requires a skill that no one can prepare you for and no textbook can teach you. However, a mother's love should never be underestimated. Its power knows no limits. Such is the case with my sister-in-law Debbie.

Every time Debbie, her daughter Courtney, and I are together, I leave them with newfound respect and admiration for how they've carved out a life for themselves that is unique and their own. Courtney has grown into adulthood, and Debbie has an extraordinary way of forging a balance between being a mother and a friend. This has created one of the most beautiful relationships I have ever seen. They go out to lunch together, get their nails done together, go to movies together, and do all the mother/daughter things that those duos do. Debbie has learned the art of caring for a Down syndrome child who is now an adult. She has faced the reality that it's no longer "her life," it is "our life" with dignity and grace. When it's necessary to draw the line between friend and mother, Debbie does it with a combination of firmness and compassion. This is really a beautiful thing to watch.

In a world where we hear about neglect and abuse almost daily on the evening news, I am fortunate to have a mother like Debbie in my life who personifies what being a mother is all about. I am especially honored to be a part of a family where I get to experience the extra special love needed to care for a special needs child. Today, and every day, I want to honor Debbie, who shows us consistently that *A Mother's Special Love* is a beautiful thing.

# The Gift That Keeps on Giving

I HAD THE PLEASURE OF COURTNEY coming into my life when she was four years old. Interacting with a Down syndrome child was not new to me because I had a cousin close to my age who had special needs as well. I learned at an early age that they were very special people and that they have a uniqueness about them that endears them to your heart.

If you have never had the opportunity to interact with a child or adult with this condition, then you are missing out. They have boundless love and compassion, and Courtney is certainly no exception. From the moment we first met, I knew we were going to hit it off.

Courtney is a kind individual with personality-plus. She is one of the funniest people you will ever meet. I tell Debbie, her mother, all the time that she could have her own TV show. The way things come out of her mouth with the innocence of a child but the wit of an adult astounds me every time I am around her. Although she is an adult, mentally she is at a much lower level. Yet at times I believe she is way smarter than many adults I know, including me.

One of the things I admire most about Courtney is her desire to serve. Put her in the kitchen and you will think you are at a five-star restaurant. Take her to a restaurant and she immediately joins the staff and starts seating patrons. Visiting a local restaurant that she and Debbie frequent is an experience in itself. She commands attention from the staff and the patrons with a sense of love and caring that is beautiful to watch.

If you ever meet Courtney, first she will show you her nails and then she will advise you that a color you are wearing matches her clothes. This is a given. Spend a little more time with her and you will discover she is an incredible person. Her personality permeates your entire being, and she quickly carves out a place in your heart that will belong to her forever. Unfortunately, not all individuals respond to special needs individuals appropriately.

One of my pet peeves is people who have negative reactions to special needs children and adults. I have occasionally shared my thoughts about their reactions with them, which often catches them off guard. Sometimes it is lack of knowledge and sometimes it is fear. Often, it's just downright stupidity. Anyone who has spent any time around special needs people understands that they come with challenges, but ultimately what you get from them is so worth it.

I have been blessed with having four special needs (not just Down syndrome) children/adults in my life. I consider myself one of the luckiest people in the world because they share with me a little part of them. Their love and compassion are truly the gift that keeps on giving, and what's more beautiful than that?

# Speaking from Their Hearts

ONE OF MY FAVORITE TIMES in the Bring Smiles to Seniors program is when we have sent a batch of cards out to the schools and they come back with the student messages written inside. Most of our cards come from elementary-school-age children, although we do have high schools and colleges involved as well. We read every card for appropriateness, and we rarely pull a card. When we do, it's usually because there is a message that may mean one thing to a child who means well, but the message would be taken differently by a senior receiving it. Receiving a message that says "I hope you don't die tomorrow" may not exactly be the way a senior wants to start their day.

When we deliver cards to the schools, the question we are asked most often is: What should the children write inside? Our answer is always the same: Let them use their imaginations and creativity and write whatever is in their hearts. Ninety-nine percent of the time the messages that come back are exactly what a senior recipient needs to hear. Children innately understand the exercise and channel the innocence they possess into messages that are heartwarming, genuine, and pure.

There is a limited amount of time that children get to enjoy that age of innocence before the world and people start to try to shape them into who they want them to be. We often force children into sports, dance, arts, or other activities simply because it is what we wanted for ourselves but never had the opportunity. We attempt to live our lives vicariously through them. Rather than let them blossom and grow into who they truly are, we try to mold them into what we want them to be. In the process, we place unneeded pressure on them that causes the innocence they were born with to disappear.

When we read children's messages, we hear their true hearts. The compassion and understanding that they convey at such an early age is truly a wonder to behold. When I am in classrooms speaking to students and I ask them how many know what a nursing home or assisted living facility is, many hands go up. It is far more likely that a child will have a relative associated with one of these communities today than at any time in previous generations. There are more of them, more people are in them, and this will only grow as baby boomers age. That also means the need that the Bring Smiles to Seniors program now strives to meet is only going to become greater.

The connection between seniors and children is powerful. That is why we have, from the beginning of the program, made connecting the circle of life our mission. Nothing can bring a smile to a senior faster than a note or a visit from a child, and we are tapping into that power to drive change. In doing so, children learn, seniors smile, and we have accomplished our mission. If we continue to let children speak from their hearts and be who they are, the world becomes a better place.

# Should What Others Say Affect Us?

WHEN I WAS A KID, I was one of those people who stayed pretty much to myself and often walked with my head down. I was always concerned about what people thought of me. I thought that everyone had to like me, or I was a failure. That's a pretty tall order for a kid, much less an adult. As you can imagine, the pressure that attitude puts on a person can often be unbearable.

Going through life trying to please everyone, often at the expense of our own happiness, is tough. Caring about every little thing people say about us and taking it to heart is even tougher. We sometimes give people power over us and we let it take hold. When we learn to take that power back from them, amazing things start to happen.

If we only knew this as adolescents, growing up would have been a whole lot easier. If we knew that people who treat other people badly only do so because of their own insecurities, we could have at least started to understand. If we knew that often the reason people said the things they did to bring us down was to lift themselves up, it would have made dealing with them much easier. When we carry this never-ending cycle into our adulthood without addressing it, we only exacerbate the problem.

I was well into my forties before I finally started to understand. I began to realize that the only way what people said about me mattered was when I gave them the power for those words to matter. I learned that only I could give them permission to do this and, unless I took it away, the cycle would repeat itself. When I took a deep look inside and evaluated the people in my life who were taking power from me, I started to prune them from my garden. It was only then that I realized that I had the need to own my power.

It's human nature to tear people down when they are doing well, and we aren't. People seem to have a hard time celebrating the successes of others when things aren't so right in their own lives. Unhappy people don't like happy people. Unsuccessful people don't like successful people. They will say whatever they can to tear people down just to feel better about themselves. Misery truly does love company.

Learning that what others say does not matter and has absolutely no effect on our lives is a beautiful thing. How successful we are, how happy we are, how content we are with our lives can only come from inside us and from no one else. We have the absolute power to determine the course of our life. Once we learn that—and believe me it is a hard lesson to learn—our life becomes very different and what others say really does not matter.

# Mean People

EVERY NOW AND THEN, a person enters your life, and no matter how hard you try to please that individual, they are just downright mean. Despite the most earnest efforts to change the dynamic, nothing seems to work. Ultimately, some people are just mean by nature.

Sometimes there comes a point in a relationship where "mean" actually becomes "bullying." It can be frustrating when you do everything possible to turn the relationship around, but nothing works. Over the years, I have discovered that those same people are the ones not used to anyone talking back to them. When someone challenges their behavior, they become uncomfortable. And the more we accommodate their bad behavior, the more they mistreat us. However, these bullies have power only if we permit it by staying silent.

Many years ago, when I lived out West, I had a client who made my life miserable. I worked in the account services area of my company where we were taught that the customer is always right, and you accommodate them no matter what. I was young and naive at the time and in my first management role. During every meeting, the client would yell and scream. If he got mad enough, he would pick up a chair and throw it across the room. Despite my best work, I could never do anything right, and he was always ready and willing to let me know it.

One time, during a conference call, my client released an expletive-laced tirade upon me. His sole purpose was to humiliate me. When I hung up the phone, I sat there in amazement, shaking. Then, I made a decision that would change how I dealt with mean people for the rest of my life: I called him back and called him out.

"Now let me speak," I said defiantly when he answered. "I've gone out of my way to ensure you and your account are taken care of. I've worked day and night to deliver the service you expect. You will not find anyone more dedicated than me! You will never speak to me like that again. If you do, I'll request to be removed from your account. And you can deal with someone new. I don't deserve to be treated the way you've been treating me. I won't tolerate it anymore."

That completely changed our relationship. He no longer berated me, he didn't yell in meetings, and he even wound up inviting me to his house for a family dinner. Once he knew that I was no longer going to allow his bad behavior, he found no enjoyment in bullying me. I also believe I earned his respect. How sad that it required a confrontation—and not my work ethic or kindness—to garner that sentiment. In that moment of standing up to him, I took away his power in our relationship.

We all have people like that in our lives. The question is whether we allow them to sap our energy and change the balance of power to the point where we are no longer equals. Or, do we take our power back and provide an ultimatum that gives them an opportunity to change? Perhaps they will show us there is no hope for them to change. At that point, we must decide if they really deserve to be in our lives. We should remind that person that we are worthy of respect. To accomplish that, we must respect ourselves first.

# It Is Never Okay

WHEN WE LOOK BACK at our lives, we find moments that stand out because they define who we are and what we believe. Unexpected things happen that change our very being and cement our opinions. One such moment for me came in my senior year of high school.

I worked two jobs in the summer before I left for college. In the morning, I worked at the five-and-dime where I had been employed for over two years. In the afternoon, I went to the new Burger King in town in hopes that I would get some fast food experience, in case I needed a job in college. It was an experience at Burger King that literally changed my life one night.

I had been at the job for several months, and I carried the work ethic instilled by my grandmother to my five-and-dime and my fast food jobs. Her "never start a job unless you are going to finish it and never do a job unless you do it right" mantra constantly played out in my head. It was all I knew. Because this was quite different than the work ethic of others in my generation who worked at fast food restaurants, I naturally stood out to management. While this may have seemed like a good thing for me personally, my coworkers didn't take it so well. They felt that management played favorites, and there was one coworker who seemed to believe that more than others.

While I forgot this person's name long ago, I can picture him like it was yesterday. He started to pick on me at work. He told me I did the job I was supposed to do simply to make him look bad. Because I was doing my job and he was slacking off, it was somehow my fault that management had a negative opinion of him. I didn't care about him enough to put out that kind of effort, but for some reason he saw things quite differently. He was determined to let me know exactly how he felt.

One night after we closed the restaurant, I went out to my car and he was still inside. As I got into my car, I felt a tug at my door as I tried to close it. Before I knew it, he was standing between me and the car door and started punching me in the side of the face repeatedly. I screamed, no one came, and eventually he just stopped and left, and I sat there stunned. Somehow, I started the car and drove through every red light in town toward home. Once I arrived, I went inside and broke down crying. My mother and grandmother drove me straight to the hospital where they discovered I had contusions on the side of my head. Fortunately, he had been hitting the hard part of my head and I avoided major damage. The hospital wanted to call the police, and my grandmother insisted that they not. I did not understand why.

Unexpectedly, the managers at work did not fire the boy and instead made us sit down together and promise that we were going to get along. Obviously, it wasn't the place for me anymore, yet despite that I stayed and worked alongside my attacker, staying as far away from him as possible until I finally left for college. Once again, my grandmother was in my head: "Never start a job unless you are going to finish it. Never do a job unless you do it right."

I found the resilience to see that job through, and most importantly I learned on that dark night in 1980 that it is never okay to put your hands on another human being. I vowed that no one would ever put their hands on me again. We are not punching bags for others' aggression—verbally or physically—and there is never a valid excuse for treating another human being that way.

I made it through that night, and although there are times when it still haunts me, I am stronger for it. Do I wish it never happened? Of course! However, I learned to turn rage into compassion, which very well could be what Grandma was trying to teach me by not calling the police that night.

# Respect

RESPECT IS SOMETHING THAT HAS been ingrained in me from an early age. Respect for our elders, respect for our fellow persons, respect for the planet, and respect for ourselves. Respect is not necessarily about who or what, it is also about ourselves and everything around us.

Every day we need to look at life as a gift—the things we have, the people who are in our lives, and even ourselves. We must care for all of them and show them the respect they deserve. People often say that respect is earned and not given. To some degree that may be true. However, I also believe that to earn respect you should show respect and lead by example.

Our family members and friends always have a choice to be in our lives. How we treat and grow the relationships leads to the amount of respect that exists between two individuals. Without respect, there cannot be trust. Without trust, there cannot be a relationship. Each person in the relationship has a responsibility to maintain the level of respect necessary for that relationship to flourish. But, in order to achieve that goal, we must first respect ourselves.

I sometimes stand in front of the mirror and take a long look at myself—not my physical appearance, but deep into my soul. I ask, based on my actions in life, how do people really see me? Do they see me as the person I want to be: kind, compassionate, generous, and loving? Or, are my actions conveying something different? I ask myself whether I respect myself enough to be able to earn respect from others. Basically, am I living a life worthy of respect? When I can answer those questions positively and know that I truly respect myself, it's only then that I can fully expect respect from others.

Finally, it's equally important to respect things. We work hard for the things we have, and sometimes we must do without to understand the importance of having. Our homes, our belongings, our cars, our personal effects, all of them are a gift of life. I truly believe that life only gives when we respect that which we are given. I question what the purpose would be if life gave us more when we fail to respect that which we already have.

If you feel there are areas of your life where respect may be missing, it's not hard to turn that around. The most important place to start is within. Once you have mastered the art of personal respect, you will find it's much easier to give and receive respect in all other areas of your life. It is when we truly learn to respect life that it becomes more meaningful for us and those around us.

# What We Say Matters

Have you ever said something in the heat of the moment and would give anything to take it back? Maybe you said something that happened to be what you were feeling, yet you did not realize the impact it would have on the person on the receiving end. Perhaps you even said it not caring about the consequences, it just happened to be what you were thinking, and you needed to get it out. I would venture to say we have all done this at one time or another.

I think about this subject a lot. I ponder moments where someone said something to me years ago, and I could picture them saying it to me as if it were today. Sometimes hurtful things that have been said to me never leave my mind. Other times, words of encouragement and good advice that I have used throughout my life are at the top of my mind. No matter what the type of message, I would guess that the majority of the people who said those things to me had no idea that 20 or 30 years later I still remember the exact words as if they were being delivered in the current moment.

Our choice of words is especially important when speaking to children. We often forget how impressionable they are and how much our words matter. What we say to them could have a more profound impact on how they develop their own self-reflection and self-worth than we even realize. The things we say to adolescents and even adults are equally important because we never stop learning.

Unfortunately, it is often the negative comments that stay with us and overshadow the positive ones. It is just how our mind operates. When the negative comments outweigh the positive, it can become even more difficult to develop our own self-worth. Getting to the point where we do not care what others think is no easy task. Therefore, it is incumbent on us to think before we speak and consider the consequences that our words may have.

There have been times when my mouth overrode my brain and what came out was not what I had intended. Once harmful words are spoken, they cannot be taken back. You can only explain what you meant and apologize. We should always consider that there is a chance that what we say may be something that the person hearing our comments may have to live with for the rest of their life. That makes it important for us to consider if our need to say what is on our mind is worth the impact it may have. It's as simple as thinking before we speak.

# Not Everyone Knows How

On one of my business trips, I was going through the Minneapolis airport when I came upon an elderly lady looking up at the arrivals/departures board seeming a bit distraught. I overheard her saying to her husband that she had no idea what to do and that the large board was just too overwhelming. I quietly approached her and tried to discern what her issue might be. She told me that this was their first time traveling. They were on their way to an Alaska cruise in Seattle and had no idea what to do. I helped her find her flight on the board, determined the gate her flight was leaving from, and then saw them to their gate. The whole encounter got me thinking.

How many things do we do in our daily routine that just seem normal and natural to us, yet can often be scary and unfamiliar to those who have never done them before? We automatically expect that whatever we know, others should know, when in reality we know nothing about an individual's familiarity with the task at hand. I often get frustrated, especially when traveling, because people don't know how to go through security, what to do with their bags, or how to move through the line. However, this situation reminded me that we aren't all regular travelers and to some, travel can be a frightening experience.

What I encountered in this situation not only applies to travel, but everyday life as well. We have become accustomed to the things we do in our daily routines. We do them over and over and most of the time could probably do them in our sleep. But not everyone has been presented with the same opportunities as we have, and that is where a little patience is sometimes needed. This is especially true when dealing with the elderly.

During this encounter, I could have just minded my business, gone on my way, and ignored the situation as not my problem. But that is not in my DNA. My interaction with that elderly couple gave them a little more faith in humanity. It familiarized them with the proper way to read the board and set them up for a smoother experience on their return, not to mention what it did for me.

# When the Heart Speaks

THERE ARE MOMENTS WHEN the heart speaks, but we are torn between whether or not we should listen. The challenge is to listen and accept that the universe is speaking to us, even though the reasons may be unclear. Such an event happened to me.

I had stopped at my local supermarket to pick up a few things around lunchtime. As I got out of my car to go into the store, I was approached by a very disheveled elderly man. He walked up to me, shaking some change that he had in his hand and said, "Could you help a guy out to get on the bus?"

Now, anyone who has ever spent time in or lived near a large city knows that this is a common occurrence. Eventually, panhandlers achieve a level of invisibility because there are so many. Sometimes I give a panhandler a few coins. Most of the time, though, the assumption is the money will be spent on liquor or drugs. This is a built-in preconceived notion, despite a lack of evidence. That day, I told the man that I was sorry, but I had no change in my pocket and went into the store.

When I got inside the store and walked up to the counter to make my purchase, a female customer behind me asked for the manager. The customer told the manager there was a "vagrant" in the parking lot asking people for money and that the store should do something about it. I understood her point, but it did not sit right with me.

After securing my purchases, I got back in my car and headed home. The closer I got to home, the more I felt the need to go back and find the man. But I suspected by the time I returned, he would most likely be gone. I also continued to question what he might do with the money. Eventually my heart overpowered my head, and I did a U-turn in the middle of the highway and headed back to the vicinity of the store.

As I entered the left lane to turn back into the supermarket, I looked to my right and saw the man sitting at the bus stop. At this point I was all the way to the left, with four lanes of traffic to my right and cars everywhere. Normally, there would be a line of cars behind me waiting to turn, but, oddly, I was alone. Suddenly, all four lanes of traffic were completely clear, allowing me to cross to the side of the road where the man was sitting.

I called him over, and he approached my window. I handed him several dollars through the car window. He looked at me and, with a tear in his eye, said, "God bless you." He told me he was waiting for the bus in hopes that he could convince the driver to let him ride for free so that he could get back home. I told him he was welcome, and I drove off.

I will never know why I was moved in that moment to do what I did. I just know that my heart was speaking to me, and I listened. On the drive home, I felt the power of compassion swelling inside me. The universe had put me in a situation where I needed to respond, and fortunately, I listened to my heart and, as a result, helped someone in the process. Sometimes, we just have to follow our heart without question when it is speaking that loudly.

Keep your eyes open, and watch for your moment today. You may find yourself doing something that you never expected or not fully understanding why you did it. But you will know in your heart there was a reason for that moment, and you will have enriched your life—and someone else's—just a little bit more.

# A Little Humanity

HAVE YOU EVER BEEN OUT and about and just observed people and wondered what their life must be like? Sometimes, we wonder based on their appearances, sometimes based on actions, and other times because of interactions with them. Our encounter with them is only one moment in time during many hours of their existence and we have no idea what may be going on in their life. Yet, that one encounter often causes us to define them for that moment when we don't really know them at all.

Sometimes, these situations have negative results and other times they are an opportunity for a positive outcome that enriches your soul. Years ago, when I was in my early twenties, I was having dinner at a Taco Bell. As I sat there having my dinner, a rather disheveled lady came in and walked up to the counter and ordered a small bag of nachos. I saw her make her way over to a table to sit down, and she started to slowly nibble on what I assumed to be her dinner. I also noticed that she had no teeth. So, biting into the hard nachos meant that she was really having to take her time.

I knew nothing of this lady—not her past or present and not her future. What I knew, however, was that there was something about her that touched me that brought out my humanity in a way that felt right. As I finished my dinner, I reached in my pocket, took out the last $5 I had in my wallet and walked over to her table and gave it to her. I then turned and walked away without looking back. You see, that moment in time and that interaction stoked a feeling of humanity and compassion that drove me to do something positive. Others may have laughed, made fun of, or even questioned why someone as disheveled as she was would be allowed to dine in the restaurant. However, I made a conscious choice to do what was right for me because that was what I had been taught.

As you go through your day, you will encounter many people in many situations that will evoke some thought inside you about them. Will you use your preconceived notions about their appearance or demeanor to guide you? Or, will you let that moment spark a little humanity in you and use it as a teaching moment to not only make yourself smile, but someone else as well. Use the opportunity of every encounter as a life lesson that what we are seeing and hearing in the moment may not necessarily be the reality of a person as they truly exist. Ultimately, our reaction to the person helps define the person that we truly are.

# We Are All
# One Big Candle

How many times in our lives have we come across people who make themselves feel better by making other people feel bad? Rather than put in the work and dedication to enhance their lives, they elevate themselves by tearing down those around them. We see this over and over in the business world and unfortunately at times in our personal lives.

On the outside, we see those who seem like everything in life is easy for them. They have everything, opportunities simply come to them, and they live a life that many people only dream of. It isn't because these people happen to be lucky. It is because they have discovered the secret of living a happy and abundant life and that becomes their mantra as they move along life's path. Alternatively, there are those who seem to live in mire no matter what they do. Yet the one thing they seem to be missing is that they do not focus and work on their own lives, rather they focus on what everyone else has. The only way they can elevate themselves internally is to blow out everyone else's candle.

Our life path decisions are totally up to us. The beautiful thing about that path is that as we work to make our lives better and promote and support people in the process, the more our lives are enriched. We are all connected in spirit, and enriching the spirit of our fellow humans makes our lives better, too. Supporting each other in our endeavors, charities, adventures, and life work strengthens our own foundation, which, in turn, gives us even greater strength to uplift others.

I've often seen people in the corporate world use others as stepping-stones to get themselves to where they want to be. For a while, they may seem successful and get to those elevated levels, but inevitably their demise comes and usually by their own actions. Those who choose to climb the ladder and take others along with them on their journey seem to be the ones who thrive the most and go on to be great leaders and do great things.

As you go through life, remember that it is important to celebrate ourselves. But it's equally important to celebrate others. While we may each have our own candle, they all culminate into one big universal candle that needs to shine as bright as our individual ones.

# Expectations

EXPECTATIONS ARE A CONSTANT PART of our thought process—those that we put on ourselves, and those we put on other people. When we have preconceived notions of what is supposed to happen, or what a person is supposed to do, when the expectation isn't met, we are disappointed.

When that happens to me, I often sit back and try to evaluate exactly what my expectations were and why they were not met. The more I do that, the more I realize that setting expectations based on how I would handle a situation usually sets me up for failure. Expecting others to deliver exactly as we would is unreasonable and sets us up for disappointment. We are all different people who handle situations in different ways.

Some people are overachievers by nature. Others deliver in their own time and way. Some are just natural born underachievers. I find if you take time to truly get to know a person and set expectations commensurate with their style, then your disappointment becomes less frequent.

Of equal importance are the expectations that we place on ourselves. I cannot tell you how often over the years I have put unneeded pressure on myself by setting expectations I could not meet. When I did not follow through, I felt unnecessary self-doubt and angst. We are not machines. We are humans with ever-changing emotions and abilities. It is important to understand our limitations and set expectations for ourselves accordingly.

Sometimes, I find it helpful to create a list of priorities in my mind or on paper. This list has all the things I expect to accomplish but prioritizes them in groups of importance. When I finish the ones that are the most important, I move on to the others, and I am left with a feeling of satisfaction. I see the list getting shorter, and I don't feel that I must do everything at once.

How we set and deliver expectations is truly a product of who we are. How we learn to adapt and alter those expectations is a product of the person we want to be. Dealing with the outside world takes more effort than it has in the past. Why set ourselves up for failure? I don't believe in expecting the worst and hoping for the best. Setting realistic expectations and then delivering on them is far more satisfying.

# Is It Okay
# to Say No?

E VERY DAY WE ARE BOMBARDED with choices to say yes or no. In-
vitations, work events, life requirements, and all the things that
come our way force us to try to balance our lives in ways that keep
everyone happy and us sane and healthy. But are we always making
the right decisions? I think the answer to that question comes at the
point when we are considering a yes or no answer and depends on
what we are using to justify our decision.

When you are presented with a question that must be answered,
how are you evaluating the answer you are going to give? Whether
the answer is a healthy one lies in the reasoning that you are using
to determine what your answer is going to be. If the answer is yes
only because you don't have the ability to say no to the other person,
then the reasoning is suspect. If the answer is yes because you've
evaluated how saying yes is going affect your other responsibilities
and your own desires, then I would guess that it's likely a healthy
answer. The more we say yes simply because we can't find it within
ourselves to say no to the person because of how they are going to
feel, the less true we are to our own needs.

I have written before that there are only 1,440 minutes in a
day. As we try and juggle all that life requires, the frequency of our
saying yes becomes unhealthy and the less time we have for the life

balance we all try and maintain. Ultimately, that means it's okay to say no. Other people's reactions to our no answer should not be the sole determination in how we are going to respond. Yes, we need to be considerate of others' feelings. However, we all know those who will always expect a yes answer from us no matter what our own needs may be.

So, my answer to the question I posed in the title of this message is yes, it *is* okay to say no. When we use the proper rationale and we balance our own personal needs, then no is perfectly acceptable. And sometimes necessary.

# We Are the Only Approving Authority of Ourselves

How much of our life do we spend trying to be someone we are not or trying to please everyone but ourselves? Rather than celebrate the unique individual we are and all that we deserve, we find ourselves trying to live up to everyone else's standards day after day. Our life becomes so mired in trying to make sure we have everyone else's approval, that we fail to realize that we really don't need it if we truly believe in who we are and our worth.

There is no commandment that says that we must mold our lives to make everyone else happy. Usually, when we make what others think of us the basis for our self-worth, we set ourselves up for major disappointment. This usually happens because many people need others to feel inferior for them to be able to feel better about their own lives, which may not be so great.

Wasting our days trying to prove our worth to others is often an exercise in futility. We become so engrossed with seeking the validation of others that we often forget to live our life for ourselves. Nowhere is this more evident than on social media. People judge themselves by the amount of "likes" on their pictures, the number of followers they have on Instagram, or the number of people who have subscribed to their page. This is something that we are likely all guilty of at some point.

We go through our days seeking approval. We want it at home, we need it at our jobs, we look for it in our extracurricular activities, and we try to find it where we can as a validation of who we are. It is only when we realize that all we need is the satisfaction that we have done our best and made every attempt to be the best we can by our own standards that we start to alleviate some of the pressure that we place on ourselves.

Our first responsibility is to ourselves and our well-being. If we are not in a good place or position, then it is rare that we would have the strength necessary to take on others. When we have placed ourselves in the position where we feel the strongest, it is only then that we realize that we don't have to prove anything to anyone other than ourselves. That gives us the life that most of us desire.

# Carry the Bags or Leave Them at Home?

WE ALL ASPIRE TO BE the best we can be. Some people work hard to achieve it, while others sit back and expect it to just magically come their way. For both, the desire is there, but the willpower to make it happen lies within us at varying degrees. One thing we all have in common is that the only way to truly fly is to give up the things that keep us from achieving our best life.

Throughout our lives, we encounter immeasurable trials and tribulations as we navigate our life path. How we deal with those trials and tribulations ultimately determines where the path will lead us next. If we see failures as learning tools and stepping-stones, the next trail may be brighter.

We find ourselves in an endless loop if we keep repeating the same mistakes. Holding onto the baggage that weighs us down only keeps us from realizing our potential. Anyone who says they always learn from their mistakes is probably not being completely honest. Those mistakes can rear their heads in ways we never even imagined. When they do, there is often no better beating than the beating that we give ourselves. The problem is, when we spend time being hard on ourselves, we add to the weights we bear, rather than letting them go and finding our true self.

Letting go of the past is difficult, and facing an unknown future can often be scary. When we face that future without all our baggage, the chance that we are going to find our way down a better life path gets that much easier. Imagine walking a mile carrying five suitcases and walking a mile with none. Leaving those suitcases at home is our best chance to truly learn to fly.

# Why Perfection?

MANY OF US WITH TYPE "A" personalities will tell you that striving to be perfect in everything we do is exhausting. We see it in our personal lives, our work lives, and even in our interactions with our social circles. When we fail to achieve perfection, we immediately feel a sense of failure because we have not achieved the level we desired. But does anyone really care how perfect we are?

Part of the issue with perfection is there is no one definition. What may be perfect to one person may be subpar to another and vice versa. We often put unneeded stress on ourselves trying to achieve what others may not perceive to be perfect in the first place. Why is it that we rely on the opinion of others to validate whether we've reached our goal of perfection when our own satisfaction with what we've accomplished is enough?

Unfortunately, many of us spend a good portion of our lives trying to please everyone else. We determine our value by the feedback from those around us. If it isn't good enough for them, then it can't possibly be good enough for us. What we sometimes fail to realize is that the acknowledgement of perfection is often withheld by others simply because they haven't realized their own perfection.

I recently read a book called *More Beautiful Than Before* by Steve Leder. In it, he talks about Canadian author Marshall McLuhan who often repeated the aphorism, "We don't know who discovered the water, but it wasn't the fish." Leder goes on to explain what he meant. "We are so close to our own lives, so immersed in our own reality, that we actually have the least perspective on it." Such is the case with perfection.

While striving for perfection may be hard, isn't it rather simple? If we've given our all and done our best, haven't we achieved perfection? My guess is the flaws we see in our work and ourselves are rarely seen by others. Why then punish ourselves for flaws that don't matter?

# What's on the Other Side of Your Wall?

D o you ever feel like your life is a little out of balance and there is something just on the other side of the wall that you can't quite get to that will bring everything back together? In your mind, you are sorting through what is out of whack, but the stress of trying to figure it out is often the very thing that keeps that balance from coming to fruition. Ninety percent of life is good, but there seems to be that last major hurdle that stands between an incomplete life and a complete one.

The normal course of life is ebb and flow. We make mistakes along the way, hopefully learn from them, and move on. Each of those moments becomes a stepping-stone to fitting together the puzzle pieces of our life plan. We often repeat past mistakes and fail to learn the lesson that life is trying to teach us, and it takes additional tries to finally overcome what seems to be holding us back. We can reach the point where we believe we finally have it figured out and life deals us one more blow that we must face. It can be related to our trial, or something totally different.

Many of us have things in our lives that helped shape the people we have become. Some are good, some are bad, and some had such a profound impact that we find ourselves dealing with them throughout life. Some things are dealt to us when we least expect it, and we find ourselves facing a new challenge that we might have never imagined. It is at those moments that we garner the strength that we need to make it through. The reality is that we do make it through. We discover an inner strength that we never knew we had and persevere despite the difficulty thrown our way.

It is not uncommon to feel like what is on the other side of the wall is unreachable. But when we start to chip away at those bricks one by one, eventually the light starts to come through and what we need begins to reveal itself. It is not an overnight process, but if we find the courage and strength to see it through, the reward on the other side of the wall can be more than we ever imagined.

# You Can Walk Through That Wall of Fear

L IVING LIFE CAN BE AN AMAZING experience if we just give ourselves the chance to take advantage of what it has to offer. We often have unfulfilled dreams, desires not granted, or wants not realized, simply because we are too afraid to take the steps necessary to see those things through. Our fear of what will be required of us, and most of all our fear of failing and not achieving our goal, serves as a barrier between us and what we want.

You often hear that nothing in life comes easy. To an extent that is true. Many times, I have made the effort to conquer that fear only to have obstacles thrown in my way that make it even more difficult to break through that fear barrier. Sometimes they are natural occurrences, while sometimes I think they are tests to determine if what I seek is truly deserved or if I am ready for what I am asking for. It is almost as if the thing I want is preceded by a test of my will and strength to determine whether I am even capable of handling what I am asking for.

A real problem arises when we've tried and failed so many times, we let fear become the only reason we no longer make the effort. We've been bitten so often that we figure it isn't worth it anymore because we believe our chance of success is so low, why even try in the first place? That is where we make our mistake. When we realize that tests and failures are what build the strength and courage to persevere, even in the face of adversity, it is only then that we have the tools we need to conquer fear and ultimately achieve our goals.

We are not always going to be successful, and we are not always going to know the reason why we were not. The road map of life is full of twists and turns that often lead us down paths we never imagined. Every one of those journeys becomes a stepping-stone to building a stronger and more meaningful existence, if we only have the will to face what may come our way and make that wall of fear less strong. Everything you've ever wanted is sitting on the other side of fear, so go for it!

# Are You 100 Percent All In?

Do you ever have those days where you feel like there are things at work in the universe that are going to change your life and you just don't know what they are? Many signs are appearing that your life is going to change for the better. You know it and believe it, but you just can't pinpoint exactly what it is. That has been me for the last couple of months.

If you continue to put your wants and desires out and truly believe that they will come to pass, the universe will find a way to deliver them to you. That is exactly what I have been doing and, under the surface, I can feel that something big is soon going to happen. The things I ask for are private and simple and hopefully not selfish. But to see them become reality would benefit more people than myself. Waiting requires patience, and sometimes patience is the hardest emotion to capture.

Throughout life, we try and fail. We also desire and never receive. Then there are times when the things we want become reality. What is the difference between these outcomes? My belief is when there is a positive outcome it is because we are all in. We truly believed our desires would become reality, and we never let doubt get in the way. We meditate or pray. And we learn that if our intentions are right and we truly believe, things happen when they're supposed to.

When there are times that we don't see our wishes come to fruition, I believe it happens for a couple of reasons. First, I believe that there is a potential unknown adverse effect that achieving our desire would ultimately have on us. We are being protected without even knowing it. Second, I believe that the problem was that we were never all in. While we certainly had the desire, we were not 100 percent committed to reaching our goal and we were not willing to put in the effort to make it happen. To succeed, we must eliminate any doubt that we can achieve what we want.

If you are striving to reach a goal in your life, take a long look at your level of commitment and see if it is enough. Evaluate where you are letting doubt into the process and then work to eliminate it. Think about the reasons for the things you asked for. If you truly believe in your heart that your request is genuine, you can see it and feel it. If you are not being protected from some adverse effect achieving your desire will have on you, then all things are possible.

# Erase Regret and
# Live a Fuller Life

H OW MANY TIMES IN OUR LIVES have we said, "I wish I had done it differently?" We feel like we made the wrong choices or decisions and then spend a lifetime beating ourselves up for them. When we made those decisions, we did so with the best information we had at the time. It may not have been the right information or enough information to make the correct decisions, but it is what we had to work with that led us to the decision we made.

Regret seems to pop up in my life from time to time, and I am learning the importance of recognizing it for the emotion that it is and then letting it go. I also try and focus on all the good things that resulted from the decision that I regret, which often negates the emotion of regret. Let me explain.

One of the regrets that tends to raise its head occasionally is the fact that I only served four years in the military and didn't see it through to retirement. I entered the military when I was 18, which means I could have retired at 38 with a lifelong pension and medical benefits. All well and good. Then I start to focus on all the things in my life that have been positive that would have never happened had I stayed on that course.

I have been fortunate to have jobs that have allowed me to have a lifestyle that I could have never experienced staying in the military. I have traveled the world and lived a comfortable life. I have amazing friends who I would not have met. Most of all, I would have never met my spouse, the love of my life, had I continued down that road. When I focus on those things, the regret that rears its head loses its power over me, subsides, and is no longer valid.

It is easy to spend our lives in regret. We constantly focus on all the decisions we should have made, instead of concentrating on all the good that has come from the decisions we did make. Living our lives in the past and filling them with regret only keeps us from living the beautiful life that we have. Erasing regret and replacing it with a focus on the positive ensures that our life is meaningful and full.

# Must Our Notions
# Always Be Preconceived?

How many times do we meet people or go into situations and even before we have a chance to experience them, we develop preconceived notions? They can be notions about whether you are going to like a person. Or, expectations that the experience of interacting with them isn't going to be pleasant. Before we even have an opportunity to get to know a person or go through an experience, we have already worked out in our mind what the person or event it is going to be like. Often, after having interacted with a person or taken part in an event, it turns out that our expectations were completely wrong.

Sometimes we don't give ourselves a chance for success with new people or situations because we are so keen on thinking that we already know what's going to happen. We set the encounter up for failure before it even occurs. In doing so, we may miss out on meeting someone special or experiencing something truly magical because in our heads we have already doomed its success.

In the past I have written about going with the flow—taking each opportunity as it comes without expectations and just letting it take us on a journey that was meant for us. Filling our minds with unfair and often unrealistic expectations and never truly giving ourselves the chance to experience the realness of the person or event in its true form is not fair to the opportunity or to us as individuals.

So often in life we allow past experiences to overshadow present realities. We already have something figured out in our heads before it even happens, and, nine times out of ten, we wind up being totally wrong. Once we have figured out what we have done, it is often too late to get that opportunity again. It makes one wonder just how many wonderful things we miss out on simply because of our preconceived notions about someone or something.

I continue to work on—and I recommend it for anyone—experiencing everything that life has to offer as it comes to us. Sometimes it's going to be great and sometimes it might not work out. But if we approach a situation with an open mind and just let things happen, we will at least know that we have given it a chance. My guess is that more times than not we will be pleasantly surprised.

# Why Is Food Often Our Most Difficult Relationship?

Looking at me, people would not normally automatically figure out that food seems to be the one thing in my life that I have difficulty controlling. When I complain about needing to lose pounds, people always say that I look fine. What they don't realize is that I see and feel it differently, and it is a struggle that many people share.

At my heaviest weight, I was 213 lbs. and 5' 10" tall. When I look back at those pictures, I wonder how I ever got there. Well, I know how I got there, I ate too much. The reality is if you eat more calories than you burn, you gain weight. It is that simple. The real question is, why do we find it so difficult to control the food that we eat?

Several years ago, I joined a concierge doctor practice where I finally got a general practitioner who spent time with me. He helped me understand my relationship with food and helped me develop a plan. Not a diet plan, but a plan to limit my intake to a certain number of calories a day. During that process, I developed a love for running and ran every morning until I eventually did my first 5k. I managed to get down to 183 pounds, which was 30 pounds lighter than my heaviest weight, and I felt great. Consequently, the doctor and I decided to move from monthly visits to quarterly and then biannual visits. Once those visits and that support stopped, I easily fell back into my old habits.

Like most people, I have many excuses. I hurt my knee, so I couldn't run anymore. I work from home, so food is always readily accessible. I like trying new restaurants. Fast food is easy for lunch. The excuses are endless. I can be on my way to the store to buy a salad and wind up with fried chicken, potato chips and dip, and of course an apple fritter for dessert! I will have just one Coke, and that turns into three. Can you see a pattern?

Anyone who has ever struggled with their weight will relate to what I am writing about. Have you ever bought the bag of chips, eaten half of them, decided to throw the rest away and then pulled them out of the garbage and finished them off, while telling yourself if they are gone you won't be able to eat anymore? How about having a freezer full of diet food readily available, but go for the piled high sandwich, chips, and donut instead? Been there, done that.

Part of recognizing an issue is being open and honest about it. Part of addressing it is admitting it to yourself. Sharing it often makes it real while hiding it allows us to continue a pattern that seems endless. When I was at 183 pounds, I looked good, I felt good, and my blood tests all returned to normal. It's a place I fully intend to get to again and maintain.

I share this story with you in hopes that if you are struggling, you know that you are not alone. I also share it with you because in doing so I no longer hide my secret in the pantry. You now also know my struggle, which means that it is impossible for me to hide it. I share my story because while we all want a healthy life for others, we also want a healthier life for ourselves.

# Our Own
# Worst Enemy

Do you sometimes feel that you set goals, make plans, create tasks, and no matter how hard you try you just can't quite seem to get there? Despite persistence and perseverance, completing the list just seems out of reach. You may finish some things, but all the items on your "to-do" list never seem to get done.

Now assume you take that same list and approach it differently. If you were to give that list to someone you knew, and they didn't complete every task, would you consider them a failure? If the answer is "of course not," then maybe you are asking a little too much of yourself and becoming your own worst enemy.

Working a full-time job and running Bring Smiles to Seniors in the mornings and evenings often results in my creating enormous task lists. The unnecessary pressure I place on myself sometimes causes me to stop and look at what I am requiring of myself, and I adjust my goals to be much more realistic and attainable. We can't add stamina to what our bodies are already capable of, and we certainly can't add more hours to a day. So why do we put pressure on ourselves that isn't necessary?

I believe everyone wants to do their best. Yet, sometimes the level of best that we have set for ourselves is unrealistic and unattainable. How often does anyone else really care that we haven't obtained an objective other than ourselves? Who is waiting there with a clipboard, doing a double check on us to make sure that we have completed what we have told ourselves to finish? Usually, it's no one but ourselves—and therein lies the possibility of becoming our own worst enemy.

If we tell ourselves that we must accomplish more than we are capable of, we only set ourselves up for failure from the beginning. When we shorten the list, accomplish what we can, and then add more as time and stamina permits, we build a firm foundation of confidence that ultimately makes us a happier and more satisfied person.

So, if you have become one of those people who have turned into your own worst enemy, you can fix it. Be as kind to yourself as you would to others. Set realistic goals and add tasks only as you accomplish others. Reward yourself for positive steps that make you successful. Most of all, be your own best friend instead of your own worst enemy.

# Exactly Like Me

OVER THE YEARS, WE AMASS a network of people who come in and out of our lives. Some are only there for a fleeting moment, and others stay a lifetime. How we invest in, nurture, and grow those relationships ultimately determines exactly what kind of relationships they will become. It also determines the longevity.

I have a handful of good friends who have been part of my life for over 20 years. They are some of dearest people in the world to me, and I wouldn't trade them for anything. However, there was a time when I had to ask myself what I was expecting from those relationships and was it realistic. When I truly focused on my expectations and did some self-reflection, I realized that some of the issues I was having were actually being caused by me.

When I give myself to a true friendship, I am all in. I am caring, compassionate, generous, and make myself readily available, sometimes to a fault. Where we sometimes get into trouble is when we expect our friends to be exactly like us. When they aren't exactly like us, we feel let down. But that they are not like us has nothing to do with them at all. All my friends have the traits I mentioned above in varying degrees, which is what makes them special and an important part of my life. Internal conflict occurs when we expect all of them to have the exact same traits that we might have, which is ultimately unrealistic and unfair.

When I truly started to focus on this and modify my expectations, I realized that each of my close friends fills a different need in my life that completes me and makes me whole. Where one may be stronger in compassion, the other is incredibly generous. Where one may always be available, others make quality time extra meaningful. We sometimes forget that they have their own lives, their own friends, and their own needs. While we would like to be the center of their world, expecting that to happen is completely unrealistic.

The more I thought about it, expecting everyone to be exactly like us makes the world a pretty boring place. Diversity in friendship and the contributions that each person provides gives us what we need to make our lives more complete. I haven't perfected the art of not expecting my friends to be just like me. It is a continuous work in progress. But recognizing the issue and focusing on it has helped me create better, healthier relationships without setting expectations that are doomed to fail. In the end, we don't want our friends to be exactly like us. Accepting them for who they are and acknowledging the unique contributions they bring to the relationship creates a foundation for strong, lasting friendships.

# Does Drive
# Equal Success?

There are many variations of the drive we have within that helps us attain our goals. Some of us push to always excel at everything. Some work to be successful but are content with balancing life and work to maintain a healthy lifestyle. Others just coast in hopes of making it through each day until they get to the next. Each path has its positive and negative aspects, and each requires a varying level of drive needed to accomplish the desired objective.

When determining whether each of those different levels of drive will be successful, it's necessary to understand what the measurement of success is. Everyone has their own definition of success, and it's easy to fall into the trap of measuring another's success by our own standards. Would a person who works 14 hours a day, lives in a large mansion, has more money than they can spend yet has no time for their family, lives on antidepressants, and never takes a vacation be considered successful? How about a person who gets up in the morning, performs their 9-to-5 job admirably, pays their bills, attends their children's extracurricular events, yet spends everything they make and lives one paycheck from poverty? Or, how about the person who gets up, goes to their restaurant server job, pays their bills, spends time at the beach, hangs out with friends, and generally enjoys life?

By their own standards, each one of these people might consider themselves successful. Yet, when evaluated by our own standards, we may disagree. Success is not something to be defined by others, but rather something we determine for ourselves. If we are maintaining the appropriate drive to get us to a level of satisfaction with our own lives and feel that we have accomplished our objectives, then by our own definition we have achieved success. The trouble begins when we compare our own measurement of success with that of others.

Success should be determined internally, personally, and within the confines of our own lives. Drive is innate. Some have more than others, and it is because of that drive that some achieve more than others. That doesn't make one right or wrong. It just means that definitions of success can vary greatly from one person to the next.

Look within and ask yourself if you are driving to be the best you can be by your own standards. Or, are you driving yourself to a level of success that is determined by others and not achievable? We often unnecessarily set ourselves up for failure by putting undue pressure on ourselves to achieve levels of success that are not possible. At the end of the day, if we can lay our heads on our pillows at night and say, "I did my best," even though we may not have accomplished all we would have liked, we have achieved true contentment and an admirable measure of success.

# To Be or Not to Be Jaded: That Is the Question

WE RUN INTO PEOPLE ALL THE TIME asking for money on the streets. It's unfortunate we must deal with this as a society, especially a society that over the years hasn't had a great track record addressing mental health and homelessness. There are times I walk right by people begging for money without even acknowledging them. Other times, I feel compelled to act on my intuition and give them something.

Years ago, I experienced a situation that put me at a crossroads about how to react to future similar encounters when spending time in New York City. Anyone familiar with New York knows it is impossible to wander the streets and not come across someone asking for money. One night, I was walking down 7th Avenue on my way from dinner back to my hotel. When in New York, I usually keep my head down, try and blend in like a local, and just go about my business. Sometimes that means you aren't exactly paying attention to where you are going, and it is very easy to bump into people along the way. On this particular evening, that is exactly what happened to me.

As I walked down the street, a man approached me from the other direction. He carried food in a Styrofoam container. I didn't see him until our elbows collided, and his food went flying all over the sidewalk. He was very disheveled and said to me, "Oh man, someone just gave me this food and now it's ruined. This was my meal for the night." Needless to say, I felt horrible. I apologized, took $20 out of my pocket and handed it to him, and asked him to please go and buy himself something to eat. He took it gladly and oddly enough didn't even say thank you. As I turned to walk away, I saw him scooping all the food off the sidewalk back into his container. He moved on and so did I.

As I was walking, I turned back to see if he was going into one of the fast food places on the street. You can guess what I saw. Yes, he had run into another person on the street, pulling the same con, playing on their emotions to get even more money. My initial reaction was to go after him, but I was in New York City, and that wasn't going to happen. My second thought was embarrassment, and I questioned whether my street-giving days were over.

The more I thought about it, the more my grandmother came into my mind. My grandmother lived her life selflessly and always helped others in need without questioning their motives. Helping others was part of our personal beliefs. I could follow her lead, or I could be jaded about my experience and in the future ignore people on the street who are in need. I realized that it wasn't worth losing my humanity over $20. If we let those who take from us under false pretenses prevent us from showing compassion, then they win, and many others lose.

Although we have a responsibility to try to avoid situations where we might be taken advantage of, when you are open to human nature, it's still going to happen. It's how we react in those situations that make and mold us into the people we are. I have no regrets that I chose the path I did that night. The man may have gotten my $20, but he didn't get my humanity. For that I am grateful, and I still get to be the person I strive to be.

# The Power of Words

SOMETIMES I JUST LIKE TO LISTEN to how individuals talk to each other. This can be at work or in social situations, and the conversations I hear are often fascinating. It is an opportunity to learn new things, observe human behavior, and see what drives people to say the things they sometimes say. Once in a while what I hear isn't all that pleasant.

When we say whatever pops into our minds, are we really taking the time to think about how what we are saying may affect the person on the receiving end? Things we say that may make us feel better because we are "getting it off our chest" may have a profound effect on the person listening, without us even realizing it. This is especially important for consideration when speaking to young people who are still learning the art of conversation and deriving meaning from what they are hearing.

When I was in high school, I was in speech and debate club. I decided that I wanted to enter the American Legion Oratorical contest. I spent hours with my grandmother practicing my speech. There were two parts to the contest—giving a memorized speech and an extemporaneous one. I loved public speaking. Even though memorizing speeches was difficult for me, I went on to win the local, district, and regional contests. Then came the state competition. I practiced harder than I ever had and wound up placing second in the state.

There was a luncheon for all the attendees after the competition, and as we were sitting there waiting for our food, our local chapter president approached us. I assumed he was going to congratulate me for placing second and representing our town well. Surprisingly, it was quite the opposite. I remember his words like it was yesterday. He said, "We were all really counting on you. It's too bad you let us all down." I still get chills when I think about that moment. Interestingly, I can't remember any other time through all my other competitions where people came up and congratulated me, even though there were many. His words seemed to erase all the good ones that had come before. Words matter, especially negative ones.

How often is it that words come out of our mouths before we realize what we have just said? Once we say them, we can't take them back. Although words may be taken out of context from what we really meant, once they have been said, they have an impact.

While I believe we all have a responsibility to share, enlighten, teach, and help people grow, we also have a responsibility to be caring, compassionate, loving, and kind. Making others feel badly about themselves serves no purpose in the long run, and we may be creating the opposite effect of what we intended. In the end, our words matter.

# Is Your
# "I Love You"
# Real?

Usually, when I visit my parents over the weekend, I go to church with my mom and aunt and listen intently to the pastor's sermon. One recent thought-provoking sermon was about love and whether we actually put the work into making love meaningful or if it is just a word that we routinely use. This got me thinking.

We use the word "love" often throughout our day. There are many things that we can say that we love: children, family, food, and travel, to name a few. But when the words "I love you" come across our lips, do we really mean them? Anyone can easily say the words. However, as the pastor pointed out, putting the work into making those words meaningful is the key to making them real.

Generally, it is pretty easy to tell when someone is saying "I love you" just because it is what they feel they are supposed to do. It's a requirement of a relationship. It's a response to something that has been said. It can even be a way to get out of a situation that should have never happened in the first place. But you need actions to back up the words to make the words real.

Loving involves caring, compassion, understanding, compromise, and dedication. It is as if you never have to say the words for someone to understand that the love is real. Simply saying the words doesn't validate the love unless they are backed up by actions that confirm them.

One of life's greatest gifts is the ability to love and even more so the ability to be loved. If we are used to bad relationships, it isn't that easy once you find true love to just let that love in. You must respect it, believe it, and let it into your heart. When we can do that, it is a beautiful thing. When we can say "I love you," and the person on the receiving end has no doubt because of our actions, that is the most beautiful thing of all.

# The Next Second Belongs to You

I N THE FEW SECONDS THAT it took you to read the title of this message, something magical happened. In less than a minute, you've reached the point in your life where, from this moment forward, you are facing the beginning of anything you want. Think about it. Everything that happened before you read this is in the past and every second after contains moments that you can make whatever you want them to be.

Have you wanted to do something to change your life, take up a hobby, read a book, start exercising or just make life something different than it's been? Well, here is your chance. That's because we control our own destiny and every second that comes next can be ordinary or extraordinary. That alone should keep us from being afraid of the future and help us embrace it, celebrate it, and put the things in place that we need to make the next parts of our life truly special.

We often spend so much time beating ourselves up for what has happened that we never give ourselves the opportunity to make life different. Either that, or we allow people to do the beating up for us and spend all our time focusing on them and not what we are capable of. Our ability to navigate our lives and leave the past behind, while using it as a guide for our future, is what determines just how "ours" our life is going to be.

I often tell my spouse as I am going to bed at night that it is one of my favorite parts of the day. The reason I say that is that I go to sleep closing the chapter on what has passed and look forward to a new morning where I can make the next day anything I want it to be. It's not because I am depressed and don't want to deal with the world. It is because I know that those few hours that come between dusk and dawn are going to reenergize me and give me the strength to make tomorrow mine.

As we strive to make our life ours, we must avoid our old enemy self-doubt. It is rare that anyone can be as hard on us as we are on ourselves and that often prevents us from moving forward. There's a powerful quote I've heard that I like to repeat: "I'm never going to say I can't do it. I'm never going to say maybe. I'm never going to say I think I can. I can and I will." That is the mantra we all need to have to make sure that the next moments we face are those that we make our own.